D0065295

YOU LOOK FINE,
REALLY

Also by Christie Mellor

The Three-Martini Playdate
The Three-Martini Family Vacation
Raised by Wolves

YOU LOOK FINE,
REALLY

Written and Illustrated by
Christie Mellor

WILLIAM MORROW
An Imprint of HarperCollins*Publishers*

HarperCollins books may be purchased for educational, business, or sales promotional use. For information please write: Special Markets Department, HarperCollins Publishers, 10 East 53rd Street, New York, NY 10022.

FIRST EDITION

Designed by Lisa Stokes

Library of Congress Cataloging-in-Publication Data

Mellor, Christie.

You look fine, really / Christie Mellor.

p.   cm.

ISBN 978-0-06-123825-3

1. Beauty, Personal. 2. Fashion. I. Title.

RA776.98.M45   2010

646.7'042—dc22

2009029200

10 11 12 13 14   OV/RRD   10 9 8 7 6 5 4 3 2 1

To my smart, talented, and beautiful sisters, Jane and Wendy

There is no excellent beauty
that hath not some strangeness
in the proportion.

Francis Bacon, Essays, *"Of Beauty"*

Beauty is the only thing
that time cannot harm.

Oscar Wilde

CONTENTS

ACKNOWLEDGMENTS

I would like to acknowledge the following friends, cohorts, relatives, and acquaintances: the inspiring women in my life, including Wendy Goldman, Susanna "Thompy" Thomson, Geri Knorr, Lisa Noyes, Bella Nestour, Martha French, Erika Schickel, Maria Bustillos, Gail Simmons, Marla Strick, Beth Von Benz, Ruth Souza, Garen Tolkin, Marge Aguirre, Alexandra Oliver, Shanté Sposato, Jane Mellor, Wendy DeRaud, Janet Travers, Alicia Brandt, Joyce George, and Diana Riesman; Amanda Peppe and the rest of the lovely ladies of Book Group; and to Raz and all my Hoffies; the stellar Leslie Daniels; the most excellent editor, Cassie Jones; my Doozy fellas and the other nice gents in my life; the bestest boys in the world, Edison and Atticus; and the inimitable, ever-supportive, always entertaining Richard Goldman.

INTRODUCTION

NOW THAT WE'VE REACHED A FABULOUSLY MATURE AGE, IT can be confusing and thorny navigating the barrage of style and beauty tips that come our way. What am I supposed to wear? Do I have to give up my baby T-shirts and low-rise jeans if I still look good in them? Is it just me, or are gyms really depressing? If only someone could give me some grooming shortcuts so I could get out of the house in five minutes without looking as if I've been living under a bridge. Do I really have to trade in my personal style for a personal stylist? It's not just fashion and beauty tips that I'm looking for: what if giant lizards take over the earth and I can't get to Whole Foods for my favorite baby lettuces? What in the heck am I supposed to do on my birthday? How in the world am I supposed to get a good night's sleep? How can I plan a delightful dinner menu for my book group? Am I really fabulous and just don't know it? Can you please give me some tips on buying wine? What if I secretly hate to exercise? Why should I start having more parties? Pickled onions: really? Where should I go for inspiration? Honestly, isn't it kind of weird that there is such a thing as a $700 haircut? Is it hot in here? No, seriously, isn't it, like, a 105 degrees all of a sudden? Also, have you seen my glasses?

All those pressing questions—and almost all of the questions in the world—can be answered by the following: red lipstick, yes, yes, fine, no, olive oil, I will explain, yes, bedtime stories, absolutely, and, finally, it doesn't necessarily have to be purple but every woman should own at least one great hat.

I say it's high time that we do less, but with more style. I say, let's spend less time fretting in front of that magnifying mirror so we'll have more time to read a little Proust and catch up on the Sunday paper. Let's spend more time riding our bikes and walking in parks and puttering in the garden, and less time worrying about whether our butts are properly perky.

We all need to celebrate ourselves just a little bit more. You might find that a cocktail is actually preferable to botulism, and that a smile really can be your umbrella. So let's raise a glass to our magnificent, modern, middle-aged selves. Then let's down the contents of that glass, and possibly pour another. Cheers! Relax. You look fine, really.

PART I

BEAUTY, FITNESS, AND FASHION

LIPSTICK, HIGH HEELS,
AND WAX, OH MY

WHEN I STARTED WRITING MY LAST BOOK, I REMEMBER BEING stuck at one point. Here I was, well out of my twenties, writing a book that presumed to tell a whole bunch of twentysomethings how to behave. Who were these mysterious twentysomethings, with their YouTube and their eyebrow studs? My husband said to me, "Well, you were in your twenties. Nothing has changed all that much." And it was true. And I am a big fan of YouTube, even if I don't have an eyebrow stud. Because, well, ow.

So here I am again, this time writing a book for women. Women of a Certain Age. Women who are over, say, forty. And I know that I can write this book because . . . not only am I over forty, I am currently a woman. And a grown-up, apparently. I know I am a grown-up woman, even though I rarely see my particular type of grown-up woman represented in advertisements or on television shows. It's like being an atheist in America. And yet, here I am.

I know women who are absolutely convinced that the job of being a woman requires at the very least a perfect, regular manicure. It requires the blow-drying of hair by a professional, the waxing of various body parts, the costly and expert shaping of eyebrows. Grooming must be done by a team of well-paid specialists. Gifts of jewelry on Valentine's Day is a given. High heels are the standard of footwear. I will admit to a certain fondness for lipstick. And yet, high heels? I like the *idea* of high heels, I just find them a ridiculous concept for actual footwear. Some women are perfectly comfortable walking in high heels, and are able to do so while simultaneously not in any way resembling ducks. I applaud their grace and fortitude.

Deep down I fear that I'm not a genuine grown-up because of my lack of grown-up footwear. I wear gallumphing Crocs and rubber flip-flops nearly year-round. I have been known to wear flip-flops with evening dresses. I cannot abide aching feet, no matter how lovely the effect might be; and I prefer to not walk like a duck. I can stand still for a very short while in high heels, but eventually someone's going to have to walk across the room to the bar or go find the restroom, and it is just not possible for me to do that in high heels. Surely it's not just me and a few scattered ex-hippies and survivalists living off the land in Northern Minnesota?

The dirty little secret is, I think Birkenstocks are comfy and adorable. This opinion, when spoken aloud, causes the most vociferous reaction among women of my acquaintance. They guffaw, they are appalled. My friend Maria is reduced to puddles of laughter. Most women I know seem more at ease with the whole stockings-and-high-heels assemblage than I, who always feels as if I'm playing dress-up. Does this mean I have gaps in my girl DNA?

For instance: I do love everything about perfume. I don't love all perfumes, because some are obviously god-awful and can render the sniffer helplessly migrained for hours. But I am utterly seduced by perfume, the idea of perfume, the thought of perfume. A dab of Chanel No. 5 at the wrist, a spot of Creed Rose Bulgari at the neck, a drop of Fracas behind the ear, or a whiff of some exotic citrus rose blend wafting off a mysterious figure as she rounds the corner; I could just eat that up with a spoon. I am similarly smitten by tools, especially a good power drill or jigsaw. Consequently, perfume and power tools have historically been one of my favorite Christmas pairings. One year I received Shalimar and a Makita drill, with the loveliest set of drill bits. Another year, Folavril and a charming pocket-screwdriver device. The following Christmas brought me a tiny bottle of Joy and a small belt sander. Plus four vise grips in my stocking! Heaven.

I find the idea of having what is politely termed a Brazilian wax absolutely horrifying. This has got to be the most painful joke ever perpetrated on the female sex, and how women fell for it I will never know. I am to believe that "too much" hair in a certain area of my anatomy is a blight, and must be removed immediately and as painfully as possible. I am to lie naked and flat on a table, while a grim Eastern European woman swabs hot wax on that very sensitive area, then proceeds to strip the hair from that area using the strips that have been placed upon the hot wax. What's next, circumcision? Ritual scarification? Bamboo under the fingernails? Have none of you people heard of razors? Did you know that fine use may be made of your leg razor, should your "area" need a little extra grooming before swimsuit season?

But perhaps you are one of those women who enjoys the hot wax, and who am I to tell you that you are completely whack? Enjoy. Am I really in the minority, as a woman who finds the whole thing uncalled for? Please send reassuring e-mail.

What else? Well, almost everything in the Victoria's Secret catalog is silly and looks very uncomfortable. I have nothing against pretty undergarments, but save me the pokey lace with the dangling gadgets and straps and the things and the foofy stuff. Can you actually wear such gear without chafing? No, you cannot. Give me a clingy black slip any day, the kind that goes equally well with a cocktail glass or a cup of coffee. The kind that won't poke me in odd places or give me a rash if I fall asleep wearing it.

Why do I find so many of these so-called female accoutrements repellent? Well, maybe because I wonder who's the one deciding what makes us feminine, or what makes us attractive. I would like to meet the gentleman who came up with that hot-wax-on-the-genitals stuff. Who thought that was a good idea? Perhaps a good friend of the guys who came up with whalebone corsets, lead-based foundation, and foot-binding.

So I'm not so much with the uncomfortable footwear and the botulism shots into the frontal lobe, but I do believe that I redeem my secret inner girl with the deft use of eyeliner and lipstick.

One of the simple joys I have in life is hunting down that perfect shade of red lipstick. When I mentioned a "certain fondness" I have for lipstick? That was sort of like William Burroughs casually remarking that he enjoys an occasional spot of heroin. Sort of like Dylan Thomas having a modest taste for spirits, or saying that Fred Astaire could cut a rug pretty well.

I am unwavering in my adoration of lipstick. Whatever girly DNA I may be lacking, whatever I'm missing in the high-heels-and-stockings department is fully represented in the lipstick department. In fact, I think there should be an actual Department of Lipstick, and I could be the president. President pro vita. I have a shameful, embarrassingly large collection. I have tracked down and cornered every micro-shade of red, and I don't believe I have missed one. If I don't own a particular shade, it's only because I had a rare and momentary flash of common sense, where I may have realized that the lipstick in question had too much blue or pink in it, and would only end up unused and rancid in the bottom of my seemingly bottomless lipstick drawer.

I have a lipstick drawer because my friend Gail came to visit me once, and actually laughed out loud when she realized that the left side of my bathroom sink was pretty much completely covered by a collection of various trays and containers (which I thought eclectic and kicky at the time) all containing tubes of lipstick. And it was a highly amused kind of laughter, but with an unmistakably nervous and horrified undercurrent, like, "you're kidding me, right? This really isn't *all* lipstick. Is it?" I was initially put out by her implied judgment, but two days later I must have been gifted with some kind of special sight, as if my friend Gail's eyeballs had been momentarily implanted into my sockets. I saw the left side of my sink. I mean, I really saw it, in a whole new light. And it was kind of embarrassing. It was as if you suddenly looked around your living room after someone's visit, and realized that you had made your friend wade through piles of newspapers and a spilled bag of kitty litter to get to the kitchen for a drink of water, which came out of the tap in rusty rivulets. It was as if I suddenly saw, in a flash of clarity, the forty-five feral cats I'd been keeping in the house. My little lipstick collection looked pathetically, psychotically, unnecessarily massive.

So I ruthlessly weeded out the old, and organized the newer, and out of sheer mortification, cleared a corner of my bathroom drawer to devote to my lipsticks. I haven't counted, but I know I made a serious dent in the lipstick population, in addition to clearing the bathroom counter. Please don't make me count. I still have more than most female mortals who aren't professional makeup artists. I'll work on it, okay?

(But in the meantime, I have a new favorite combo to aid me in achieving that elusive, perfect matte red: Fire Down Below by Nars topped with MAC Ruby Woo. Seemingly impossible to remove, deliciously like that slightly dried-out perfect red you found in the bottom of your mother's purse when you were five years old.)

TRY THIS, I DID!

If I own an unmentionable number of lipstick tubes, I am guessing there are one or two of you out there who also have private and enormous stashes of lipstick. Or mascara. Or eyeliner, or foundation, or blush. We put on our lipstick (or mascara, or eyeliner, etc.) as we would armor, rarely going an hour, much less a day, without spackling on our signature shade. Maybe I'm the only one in the world who rarely leaves the house without an indelible coat of red lipstick. Maybe this doesn't apply to you at all, because you're perfect just the way you are, and you look all fresh and natural without the aid of cosmetics. Well, lucky you. Please take this time to go have a nice cup of herbal tea and we'll meet you back here for the next chapter. But if you are like me, I recently found it very helpful to try going a week without lipstick. Or you can try it just for a few days, if a whole week sounds like too much. Now, I'm not suggesting that you actually give up your lipsticks forever. What in heaven's name for? But recently, I went ten whole days without putting on my usual red lipstick. Nothing on my lips but some Burt's Bees lip balm. Bare naked lips. It was a little scary at first, but I think it was an important first step in acceptance. Acceptance of my face just as it is, without the thing that I thought was giving me strength to face the world. I like having a signature look; I like being the woman in the red lipstick. But just as I believe it's valuable to spend a few weeks from time to time without alcohol, or sweets, or saying bad things about people, it was a revelatory experience spending ten days without my camouflage. And blond ladies, while you're at it, put down that dark mascara and try batting your white-blond eye fringe for a week. You have no idea how cool that looks!

YOUR LIPSTICK PRIMER

That said, here is a lot of what I know about lipstick. And trust me, I know a lot:

- When you're on the go without a small mirror in your purse, use your cell phone! The reflective surface of the screen will give you just enough reflection to apply a touch-up coat, in case you can't get to a ladies' room. If you have no cell phone, you must live a refreshingly quiet and contemplative life, and I applaud you for it.

- Some may disagree on the etiquette, but I think if you're at a restaurant table and in a hurry, you may use a knife as a mirror, but only for taking a quick look to make sure your lips are still where you left them, and to assist you in not streaking your new Lancôme across your face.

- A lip pencil is not really necessary. Sometimes I use a lip pencil, but not all the time. If I do use one, I use it to make a nice outline, which I then fill in. The lip pencil is like putting down a solid matte base coat under your exterior paint. You can even substitute lip pencil for lipstick, with a dab of lip balm underneath to give it some glide. Never line your lips in pencil without filling your lips in, because you'll just end up looking like a five-dollar storefront psychic. If this is the look you hope to achieve, well, that's how you do it. (Don't forget some teal-blue eye shadow and gobs of lashes, too! Really, that looks great. Now adjust your turban, a little to the right. That's it!)

There is another school of thought entirely on the lip pencil question. Some say that lip pencil should only be applied *after* you've applied your lipstick, which will help the pencil glide on more smoothly and helps even out the contour of the mouth.

- It's not necessary to be too, too exact when you apply your lipstick. Unless you have the most beautifully shaped lips in the universe, then by all means, be exact. But otherwise, I think it's a good idea to apply your lipstick, blot, apply another coat for good measure, then take your finger or a cotton swab and lightly smooth the outside line. The edges won't look as harsh then, and you can even out the shape if it ended up a little lopsided.

- Here's a good trick: after you've applied your one or two coats of lipstick, take your finger or a rolled-up tissue and wrap your mouth around it as you would a drinking straw. This will theoretically prevent your lipstick from accidentally appearing on your teeth, which is never a good look.

- You know those old butter dishes people used to use to serve butter at the dinner table? A small, butter-stick-shaped saucer with a butter-stick-shaped dome to cover the butter? Well, I have a few of these that I've found at thrift stores, and I think they make fantastic lipstick holders. I put them in my bathroom drawer, and they each comfortably hold about ten to fifteen lipstick tubes. I store my lipsticks upside down with the

label facing up, so that I can easily spot my MAC
Dubonnet among the MAC Retro, MAC Mystic,
and Chanel Russet Moon.

- Sometimes you arrive at a party sporting your
darkest, reddest, vampiest lipstick, but as the night
wears on, so does your lipstick. After nibbling
on hors d'oeuvres, sipping cocktails, and possibly
eating dinner, you will want to reapply. But
sometimes your lipstick has worn off in a nice way,
and it's late, and you just don't want to go back to
your original grand-entrance look. That is why
I always bring an alternate lipstick in my purse.
It's usually a lighter color, and it's usually more
balm-like and less like a matte spackle. It's usually
something I can swipe over my lips without the
aid of a mirror, while I'm heading to get my shawl
(because the air has gotten a little chillier but I'm
in the middle of a good conversation and I don't
want to miss too much because I had to wait in
line for the bathroom to reapply my lipstick).

- I often use the back of my hand as a blotter, but
I don't blot the entire surface of my lips, just the
inside. People may wonder why you appear to be
kissing your hand. Why shouldn't you kiss your
hand? You deserve a few extra kisses. Kiss away,
kiss with abandon. Then rub the back of your hand
with the back of your other hand to rub out the

blot line and impart a slight pinkish glow to your hands.

• Don't be afraid to mix colors!

• To become a true lipstick professional, know how to put lipstick on in your sleep, with your eyes closed, and with one hand tied behind your back. Practice with clear lip balm, gradually moving up to light colors, then to dark. Practice at home with your eyes shut, practice while you are being ferried in a car, or riding in a public conveyance. Soon you will easily be able to whip out your favorite lipstick tube and apply lipstick without the aid of a mirror or any reflective surface, without subsequently looking as if you have applied your makeup with your foot after a strenuous happy hour.

In an economic downturn, lipstick sales go up. Somebody did a study somewhere proving that fact, but it shouldn't have taken an elaborate study to figure that one out. Lipstick is one of the most inexpensive fixes a girl can buy when times are tough. The perfect lipstick (and trust me, I have found literally hundreds of "perfect" lipsticks, it's not a problem) will dress up last year's ratty wardrobe and gussy up your fat pants. A good red lipstick will pull together a less-than-stellar assemblage immediately. A new tube of lipstick will perk you right up. But please, I beg of you, don't make my mistakes. Know your limit. Too much of any good thing is still too much.

MAGNIFYING MIRRORS:
A NECESSARY HORROR

A magnifying mirror is indispensable to have on hand when you need to take a closer look. It will aid you in removing an eyelash stuck in your eye, it will help you when you want to remove a few stray hairs from your eyebrow area, or check out that weird red spot in the middle of your forehead. However, one may take the magnifying mirror–gazing too far. It's easy to start out with the "how did those three hairs get on my chin! Oh my god, have I been walking around like that?" and wind up staring in horror as we discover new lines, new veins shot through our eyes, hairs coming out of moles we've never seen before, and mustaches we never knew we had.

Yes, it's helpful for applying eyeliner, but just remember, before you fall down the rabbit hole of magnification, that you don't need to use your magnifying mirror to apply the rest of your makeup. Your friends, in all likelihood, do not have X-ray vision. Many of them are incrementally losing their eyesight, just like you. Those who still have the perfect use of their eyes are probably not going to use their gift of sight to inspect your upper lip, unless you have accidentally left some food there.

Presumably no one is looking at you with a magnifying glass. If they are inspecting you with a magnifying glass, they probably wear a tweed hat and call themselves Sherlock. Your friends and acquaintances won't necessarily focus obsessively on that one area between your eyebrows, even though you may be spending hours in that very pursuit. People generally tend to take in the whole picture.

Think of yourself as a lovely impressionist painting. People, by and large, don't stare at the brushstrokes in one corner of the canvas; they stand back and assess the painting. When people look at you, they will notice the whole pleasing effect of your features working together. They'll probably notice how your eyes crinkle up in a lovely way when you smile, and how your hair looks nice like that, and what a good laugh you have. They will probably be more interested in what you're saying than how your makeup is applied, although if it looks as if you applied it with a trowel, they may notice that. You don't need to apply your makeup with a trowel, and if you don't stare too long in the magnifying mirror you'll apply it with a much lighter hand. Step away from the magnifying mirror.

Instead, give yourself a brief overview in a regular mirror, preferably one with a natural light source nearby. Of course use the magnifying mirror, if you need it; but use it judiciously. Make it your friend. It will be there for you when you need to do the detail-oriented stuff, but do not let it mesmerize you into thinking that your eyebrows could really use some plucking, because what looks like "really could use some plucking" to a magnifying mirror looks like regular eyebrows to a real mirror. And if you believe the magnifying mirror, you will find yourself with two very thin, very surprised-looking arches hovering above your lovely eyes. So, don't use the magnifying mirror to shape your eyebrows, only to get a few stray hairs.

Magnifying mirrors are handy, however; I treasure mine, and wish I could find a small one to take with me when I travel, because they're especially useful if you're away from home and out of your usual routine. Things start . . . growing in places.

Things do perhaps need a little plucking and trimming and taming. But restrain your hand, and don't be overzealous with the plucking. Remember that to normal eyes, you look fine, really.

FOUNDATION: YOUR OWN
PERSONAL VINYL SIDING

When I was younger, I loved wearing a nice makeup foundation. I'd wear a pale ivory in the winter to accentuate my pale winter skin; for summer parties, something a little more Ava Gardner bronze-y, to go with my dark red lipstick. When you're younger you can really pile on the makeup, and if it's done right it will look showy and dramatic. When you're older and you pile it on, you run the risk of frightening small children or getting picked up for soliciting. Liquid makeup tends to sit in crevices, and powder-based makeup tends to seek out hidden wrinkles and highlight them.

If you're used to slathering it on, it may be time to start applying it with a lighter hand. Dab a few dots just around your nose and the bottom corners of your mouth, or anywhere your complexion might need a little evening out. Then try mixing a few drops with a little moisturizing cream (or sunblock, by day) or a few drops of water, and lightly smooth the diluted foundation over the rest of your face.

THERE'S SOMETHING
WRONG WITH YOU!

AT THE GROCERY STORE, AT THE MUSEUM, AT THE BOUTIQUES, I often find myself face-to-face with a fair number of women who I am certain had their faces reconstructed after terrible accidents or falls, or perhaps a Beverly Hills gang rumble; and then I realize, no, it wasn't a barroom brawl; these women paid a doctor a truckload of money to look like that. They made appointments to have that done to their faces, voluntarily. You know the face I'm talking about; everyone is pretending that it's a good idea: the exaggerated cartoon cheekbones robbed from the grave of Elke Sommer, the mouth that is stretched from ear to ear in a Grinch-like rictus, the wide, surprised eyes whose lids don't quite come to a close, the lips that look like shiny, pink, overstuffed satin pillows. Or the latest trend: the slightly simian, face-forward puffiness of the highly implanted and injected. Lips and cheekbones built on top of your regular face, so that it looks as if you're leaning forward a little. Yes, your face is as pink and smooth as a baby's butt. Yes, you look like you could be a twenty-two-year-old. Just not necessarily a twenty-two-year-old human.

Of course, I live in Los Angeles, but this is no longer just a phenomenon of Hollywood. This unfortunate trend is trickling down to not only younger actresses but nonprofessionals as well; women in their thirties and forties who were just starting to look really interesting and now look eerily like one another, or Melanie Griffith. Ultra-thin and extra-collagened women are seeping into the mainstream, cheerfully aided by mass media, makeover shows, and marketing.

"I'm very, very angry."

"I am just LIVID."

I am FURIOUS!"
(Also, I'm fifty-five years old)

"I'm ENRAGED."

Yes, many of us are reaching an age when we are taking a serious look at our faces. The jawline is just a little slacker than it used to be, those vertical lines between the eyes seem to have taken up permanent residence, and we start asking the questions: would I prefer to have lips that look like an inflatable duck or lips that look like two breakfast sausages? Shall I opt for the perennially surprised eyes, the giant expanse of frozen forehead, or just go for the giant cotton-stuffed cheekbones that seem to be so popular? And should I go for the whole face-lift, and if so, what kind should I get—the kind that stretches your mouth to your earlobes, or the kind that makes you look like an Asian space alien? The choices are seemingly endless, and yet all so frighteningly unnatural.

Well, I have a trick that's better than Botox, and you will think it's a joke, but it is really not a joke. It's just a little trick I learned when I started making fun of women who had gone a little overboard with Botox. And what I discovered is that you can use your own muscles to do the same thing Botox does, but without having to endure botulism toxin painfully shot into your face, just a few inches away from your brain. Not that having botulism toxin painfully shot into your brain area doesn't sound like a fabulous idea and a really great way to be beautiful, but, you know, just in case you wanted to try something a little less scary-sounding, while saving hundreds of dollars.

So here's what you do: first of all, just relax your face. You can do this, all by yourself, honest! Unknit your face, unfurrow your brow, loosen your jaw. Then you sort of pull your scalp back with your scalp muscles, which will make your forehead feel all open and stretched. Think serene thoughts. Imagine light oozing out of your pores and the crown of your head. See your face, not frozen but filled with serenity and stillness. It works, I swear. Lift those muscles that cause you to "smile" and you will suddenly radiate a certain indefinable peaceful, happy something. Your forehead will look open and untroubled.

I know, you're all, "Right, think happy thoughts. That'll work." But it will! Along with a little extra sleep, a little flax oil, and a handful of almonds every day, this simple exercise will remind your facial muscles to not fall into those bad habits; it will remind your brow not to knit and your forehead not to get all scrounged up with worry. And it will start feeling normal after a while, and pretty soon you won't want to scrunch your face up and fret about stuff over which you have no control.

Use your fingers to smooth those worry lines in your forehead every day. Gently rub up and out from your brows to your scalp. It feels really good, and takes the creases out. And if your hair is long enough, pull your hair back in a ponytail for an instant face-lift!

"Thinking happy thoughts" isn't just a cheap bromide; the regular practice will actually result in fewer wrinkles, smaller pores, brighter skin, a pleasant sense of well-being, and possibly world peace.

FOR THAT LITTLE EXTRA LEG UP:
EXERCISES FOR AN INSTANT FACE-LIFT

My friend Thompy, who is a gorgeous and talented actress, learned of these weird, fabulous facial exercises from a makeup artist named Dallas Hartnett, who swears by them for toning the neck and jowly bits. Alternatively, you may choose to spend tens of thousands of dollars for the opportunity to endure painful and risky surgery, which could result in an oddly implanted, vaguely lumpy, duck-billed face, which of course is another fine option. But just in case you're still weighing the pros and cons, you can do these toning exercises a few times a day while you're deciding! And maybe by the end of the month, you'll look at your taut, glowing face and think, "Hm, maybe I'll wait to get cut with a scalpel around the hairline and have my facial skin peeled back, exposing the raw sinew and bone. For now, anyway. Although it does sound like fun!"

ALIEN I

Lift your chin slightly, as if you're looking at a distant star a little higher than the horizon. Jut your lower jaw forward so it looks like your lower teeth are almost biting your upper lip, or you're trying to touch your lower teeth to your nose, or you're attempting to hide your upper lip in a little pocket behind your lower teeth. This will make you look like THE ALIEN. This will make you look like a scary, scary monster lady, so don't do this fabulous facial exercise around any small children. Relax slightly, then bite. Relax, then bite. Slowly, methodically, gently jut your lower set of teeth out and up toward your nose. Keeping your chin lifted, slowly turn your scary alien face to the right. Slowly turn your scary alien face to the left. Then back to the center. You will FEEL THIS tomorrow, I'm not kidding. In your neck, and your jowly areas, there are muscles and tendons that have been kind of taking it easy for a few years. So start slowly, but do it a little bit every day; do a few in the shower, in the kitchen, in the car. Be aware of frightening fellow motorists, if you attempt this exercise while operating a motor vehicle.

ALIEN II

This facial exercise is very similar to "The Alien I," but this time you will jut your lower jaw forward, then shift your jutting lower jaw to the right, then the left, back and forth, swiping your lower set of teeth just across your upper lip. It will feel odd at first, in those alien tendons on either side of your neck. But do the back-and-forth for a few minutes a few times a day and you will keep your jawline supple and your neck taut. Or perhaps your jawline will be taut, and your neck supple. Either way, things will be a little more taut and supple around here, and that's fine with me, because honestly, who wants to have to wear a turtleneck in the middle of summer, right?

YOUR WARY ACQUAINTANCESHIP
WITH FOOD

PITY THE POOR CELEBRITY WHO GETS SPLASHED ALL OVER THE covers of the tabloids if she gains twenty pounds. She is shamed for the roundness of her belly and derided for her dimpled thighs. She is soundly ridiculed for packing it on and really letting herself go. Six months later, a photo of her hits the cover of the *Daily Mail* and makes its way around the Internet. She is gaunt, emaciated, and it's whispered that she is starving herself to death for her career. WTF? (As the kids say.) No, really. What the . . . ? (As the Three Stooges say.) I mean, people, can we make up our minds here? Is it possible that women are getting a few mixed messages?

It's only slightly easier for those of us who are not required to be in front of cameras on a regular basis. The minute we start accepting our bodies, really coming to terms with our own singular beauty, we're sitting in the dentist's office reading about some woman who is a foot taller than we are and yet, remarkably, weighs thirty pounds less. She is, insanely, described as having "womanly curves." She looks like Bambi, yet is lauded for being so much more robust and healthily well-rounded than some of her fellow models. And yet, you search for the womanly curves. You think to yourself, "I thought 'womanly curves' were those things I have around my hips that make my pants tight."

I've always been adamant about the significance of the celebratory nature of food; it's an important part of gathering with friends. Eating and drinking are two of the greatest agents for social interaction ever created. I think putting out a plate of cheese, some grapes, and a crusty baguette for a visiting friend is an act of love and kindness. Eating real food is one of the joys of life.

And eating healthfully is a delightful and nurturing way to live; but please, don't become vocally obsessive over every bite that enters your bodily temple. Bread will not kill you; and stating this as a fact while you are figuratively breaking it with friends or family is simply in poor taste. Perhaps white flour and processed sugar don't agree with you in particular. Too much of either isn't good for anyone. But making a disgusted face or a smug remark as the dessert is being passed is just not nice. No one cares that you'd prefer to avoid gluten. No one needs to know that you are wheat-sensitive unless you are in danger of your throat swelling closed in the middle of a dinner party. If your hostess makes a point of asking why you have no noodles and bread on your plate, simply say that you wanted to make enough room for all the other good food. If there is no other food but pasta and bread, then serve yourself a very small portion and tell her you had a huge, late lunch.

I regaled my friend Martha with my entire treatise on the subject. My friend Martha is a nurse. She is a willowy, attractive, intelligent, no-nonsense woman; I am guessing she is one of the best nurses on the planet. She's never been *my* nurse, we've only been friends since before we were born, but I'm just speculating. So Martha listened patiently to my diatribe, and then said, "Well, that's true. But you still need to have a healthy BMI." Right. Of course. A healthy BMI.

As much as I've always secretly fancied myself an impish gamine—sort of like a slightly squatter version of Audrey Hepburn—I have always rebelled against the extreme, stick-figure ideal of beauty. And in my rebellion, I developed something akin to reverse anorexia. Reverse anorexia is a mind-set where you look in the mirror and think you look fine. No matter what. That seems normal and healthy, right? Well, it is, to a point. You get really, really good at disguising the extra twenty-five pounds with a stylish combination of clothing, except that suddenly, you have fewer and fewer articles of clothing that actually fit. And then you start wearing cumbersome shawls. Even in the middle of summer.

I had a vague idea of what "body mass index" was, and summarily dismissed it as some sort of fad. But when I got home, I did that calculation on the computer where you check your BMI, and I realized with a sinking feeling that, in fact, my BMI exceeded what was considered healthy for my height. Which is especially horrifying because I always secretly add that extra half-inch to my height. Because, you know, I just sound less like a midget that way.

So I arduously, and over the course of a year or so, changed my relationship with food and exercise. (Okay, I'm still working on my relationship with exercise. Our relationship is fraught. I find exercise incredibly demanding. But just when I think it's not going to work out, and want to break it off, I realize how good it is for me. Damn you, exercise!) So slowly, painstakingly, I managed to get myself just on the other side of the bad BMI line, and this is what I think:

I still love that good food is an important part of gathering with friends. I still believe that eating and drinking are two of the greatest agents for social interaction ever created. It doesn't, however, have to be the only exciting thing you have in your life.

Moving your body around from time to time is really, really important. I love to move around, I do. I just forget. And when I forget, I end up sitting around a lot, and then I wonder why I'm so cranky and feel so out of sorts and elderly. I have great ambitions to take a kayak out to the channel and spend an hour rowing; I think about going to a dance class. I picture myself running two miles, and sailing to Hawaii. But suddenly I look up from my computer and it's five o'clock, and dinner needs making, and someone or other needs feeding, and I manage to stretch my legs, but I only run as far as the kitchen, to make myself a cup of tea and get dinner started. This is not the aerobic workout generally recommended by doctors. I really need to do better. And perhaps you do, too. So I'm going to make it really easy for you, as easy as possible. And then maybe we can both grow up to be healthy, strapping, energetic women.

BE YOUR OWN
PERSONAL TRAINER

SOME OF US DON'T ADORE GOING TO OUR LOCAL GYM, WITH its monthly fees, indifferent employees, and bank of televisions that seem to all be tuned to Fox "News." For some of us, it takes a friend to actually remove us bodily from the house and walk us there. Sometimes we need our hand held. Sometimes we'd rather just opt out altogether, preferring to spend that monthly gym membership on, say, the gas bill, or food for our children.

Some of you love going to the gym. Some of you can afford to go to nice gyms, where good-looking people are helpful and you have a steam room and a sauna. Perhaps even a cedar-lined sauna, and a steam room that doesn't smell like old socks and black mold. Some of you look forward to going to the gym; in fact, some of you can hardly wait until your spinning class starts, followed by hot yoga. And I am so happy for you. But for those of you looking for an option other than the stair climber that makes you just want to climb three-hundred floors and jump, my lovely and talented pal Erika has devised the most ingenious alternative to a gym membership. The Backyard Workout Wonderland!

Yes, you still have to drag your sorry butt out of bed to work out, but you won't have to go very far. Yes, for very little outlay of cash, you can have your own home gym! No, you don't need a giant treadmill that will only end up as an expensive clothing rack. That's why we have "sidewalks" and "parks." But your very own Backyard Workout Wonderland! will provide a stimulating and healthful workout on those days you just don't want to go farther than your own backyard. Or in case you live someplace that has no sidewalks or parks. If you have no backyard, well, I'm just going to call it a Backyard Workout, because it is nice to do outside. But you can easily make this a Living Room Workout Wonderland!, or an Apartment Hallway Workout Wonderland!

I've been hearing about my friend Erika's backyard gym (she doesn't know that I've taken to calling it "The Backyard Workout Wonderland!" yet, I think I'm going to surprise her) for months, so this morning I rode my bike over to her house to try it out. And it was amazing! Here's what you'll need to create your own . . .

BACKYARD WORKOUT WONDERLAND!

    1 mini-trampoline
    1 hula hoop
    1 set of 10- to 12-pound weights
    1 jump rope (or length of rope to use as a jump rope)
    1 yoga mat
    1 giant inflatable ball, as in *The Prisoner* (optional)
    A deck of cards
    Music, music, music

Start on your mini-trampoline with some simple, gentle bounce action. If you don't have good sneakers, you should probably get some. But don't let the lack of good sneakers stop you from working out in your Backyard Workout Wonderland! Your mini-trampoline will cushion your landing, so you can really do this whole workout in bare feet. Bounce, and bounce, and bounce some more. Then move up to the universally beloved jumping jack. Raise your arms above your head to raise your heart rate, do some twists and raise your knees. At first it will seem totally easy, then all of a sudden you'll think, "Wow. My legs. Dang. Haven't felt that for a while." At this point, you need to keep going, apparently. Just for a little while longer, until you feel your breath getting a little heavier, and your legs getting a little tinglier. When you look down at your calves and go "ow," you may dismount your mini-trampoline. But you'll be back.

Next, a few rounds with the hula hoop. If you haven't operated a hula hoop since third grade, it's as easy as you remember it being. And if you have never operated a hula hoop, just swing it around your middle and keep it there by madly rotating your hips in a circular manner. Once it's got a rhythm, you won't have to swing your hips quite so madly, just in gentle circles. The real trick *is getting it to go in the other direction.* Good luck!

Next, do some jumping with the jump rope, which, in case you haven't used a jump rope since third grade, is a lot harder than you might remember. The stepping jump, with one foot at a time, isn't so bad. But there is a definite degree of difficulty in the actual two-footed jumping. Just bear with it, and try not to trip all over the rope, and your feet. Jump until you start getting sweaty; then jump some more. If you have room in your backyard/patio/hallway/apartment balcony, do some skipping jump rope. Advanced jumpers: Hot Peppers! Then reward yourself with a nice swig of water.

My favorite of all of Erika's fabulous Backyard Workout exercises is her version of fifty-two pickup. Remember those great games of fifty-two pickup when you were a kid? If not, this game requires that you drop your entire deck of cards. All fifty-two of them. Jokers too, if you have them. Just drop them. Do not fling them; simply drop them in front of your feet. Then, keeping your back straight and your knees squarely over your feet, squat down and pick them up. One by one. No, I'm not kidding! Do it once with your feet facing forward, then do it again with your feet forming a "V" shape. If you need a little break in between sets, do some bouncing on the trampoline. Turn up the music and rev up your trampoline jumping.

Then lift some weights to strengthen your upper body, perhaps ten to fifteen repetitions of something for the biceps and the triceps. Then lie on your mat and do this thing where you pass the giant *Prisoner* ball back and forth from your outstretched hands to your feet. Then do some push-ups, and a few crunches, and some backward push-ups for your triceps. Erika calls triceps "batwings," which I find hilarious. If you start thinking about "batwings," it will make you want to do more exercising of your triceps. If the music is getting good, dance around a little. Another go at the mini-trampoline, another set with the jump rope or deck of cards. If you feel sufficiently sweaty, do some stretching and drink a carafe of water. You will feel so good later on, if you don't already.

Your little Backyard Workout equipment can be kept all

together under a bed, or, if you tip the trampoline onto its side with the hula hoop and put the other stuff in a sturdy plastic bag, you can keep it all outdoors, leaning against a wall. (Except for the yoga mat—you might want to keep that indoors. Spiders. I'm just saying.) Just don't hide your Backyard Workout equipment too well; you need it to be accessible. You need a visual reminder to use your Backyard Workout Wonderland! In fact, the best thing is to find a little corner where you can keep your trampoline on a semipermanent basis. That way, when you're dragging yourself around with a bleary eye and a cranky spirit, you'll look over and see it. And you'll think, "Oh yeah. That'll make me feel better." And you'll know that you really don't have to do much more than throw on a few supportive undergarments and put on some music in order to be off and running. You'll think, "What the hell, I might as well do that," and before you know it, your calves are getting that tingly feeling and you're moving up to twelve-pound weights.

The important thing, if you've been a sedentary person for a while (er, note to self), is to start moving a little bit every day. Just move. Jump on that trampoline, dance around in your underwear, do push-ups off your wall and calf-lifts when you take a shower. If you can get friends to join you for regular walks, that's even better. And then you can start adding short sprints to your walks, and lunges (which are a lot less embarrassing to do in public if you're with a friend), and skipping, which is always fun to do and makes other people happy just to watch it.

Here's a story about skipping that makes *me* happy:

My friend Adam was having a very crazy and stressful week at work. He hung up the phone with a colleague in New York, took a deep breath, closed his eyes, and asked himself what he should do. And this is what he heard: "Skip down the halls of the office."

This is what Adam wrote to me:

So, I just skipped for a good three minutes up and down the halls of my offices. People looked at me like I was a nut, but I kept skipping. By the time I was done and I skipped back to my office, I realized there were six other people skipping right behind me. Wow, that was amazing. What a great way to wind down a stressful week.

Can you imagine? It shouldn't take such a great amount of bravery for a grown-up to skip down the hallway, or to sing out loud while walking down the street, which is something my friend Steve does when he feels like it. (I believe "When You're a Jet" is his preferred number.) Steve is not a professional performer, by the way, nor is Adam seven years old. I am working my way toward this kind of fearlessness. I mean honestly, if I can't do it now, when will I ever get up the gumption?

THE BEST WORKOUT

The best workout in the world is to have my friend Wendy Goldman come over. Because when you get together with Wendy, you end up laughing, and laughing, and laughing, really hard. So that's a great workout. But if you can't have Wendy over, like, if you don't know her and you think it would be awkward to track her down and ask her over for coffee or something (she really likes coffee), then find a friend who makes you laugh really hard. Preferably someone you can laugh *with*, rather than laugh *at*.

If you don't have such a friend, then just find a really good friend and invite her over to watch a funny movie, like the Marx Brothers' *Duck Soup,* which has a way of making you fall out of your chair. (My father and both of my children have all literally fallen out of their chairs while watching this movie, at one time or another, so I know it can happen.)

If you get tired of laughing, but you still want to feel really good in a way that doesn't involve sex or chocolate, you can try this with your friend: think of everything you like about this friend. Think of everything you love about this friend. And have your friend think of everything she likes and loves about you. Hopefully you will have five good ones each. Then trade compliments, one at a time, back and forth. Whoever is receiving the compliment can't say ANYTHING, except maybe at the end you're allowed to say "Awww," or "Thank you!" Your heart will grow two sizes, I swear. But it's pure muscle.

A MAGIC WORKOUT IDEA

Here is something I read in *Self* magazine, which I normally don't read, but sometimes a girl gets all caught up surfing the Internet, especially when procrastinating a deadline. One link leads to another, and pretty soon it's dark outside. But sometimes you come across a sparkly gem of information, and in this case I might have struck gold. For those of us who are less than thrilled at the prospect of literally pounding the pavement in our running shoes and pair of saggy sweat pants, some perky lady at *Self* magazine swears that this exercise is the actual equivalent of jogging for sixty minutes. And you know what? I believe her!

I just do. She seemed so sincere. I want to believe. So here is her recipe for a sixty-minute jog in a quarter of the time. It takes fourteen minutes to do, and you can alternate days with your mini-trampoline and weight lifting. Who doesn't have an extra fourteen minutes? I probably have at least an extra half hour, but don't tell that to the perky magazine lady; she looked like she could hurt a person if she wanted. She could hurt you badly and smile the whole time.

Okay, so here's what you have to do: run as fast as you can for thirty seconds, followed by four minutes of slow jogging or walking. You'll do the thirty-second fast sprint four times and alternate it with the four minutes of walking or slow jogging, which you'll do three times. A total of twelve minutes walking/ jogging, and a total of two minutes all-out sprinting. That sounds like something that almost everyone can do, and you don't need special equipment or a track, necessarily—unless sprinting on pavement will bother your knees. But the four-minute walks broken up by the fast sprinting seems like an easy way to get the blood flowing, to trick the body into exercising. And the thought of actually doing it doesn't scare me as does the thought of *running for an entire hour,* which makes me instantly want to curl up with a blanket and a good book. I can't imagine running for an entire hour unless I was actually being chased, and the person/ monster/alien chasing me would have to be heavily armed and/ or breathing fire. Then again, it might work to visualize being chased by an armed, fire-breathing alien monster just to get you off and running. Oh my god, it's huge, and it's breathing FIRE!! RUN FOR YOUR LIVES!!!

BUT WAIT!

"Wait!" you say. "I go to the gym all the time. In fact, I go every morning for about four hours. I am a gym animal. I know how to work every machine in there, plus I have a private trainer once a week, after my fitness boot camp, and three times a week I go to an evening power yoga class, and on the weekends I run ten miles in the mornings. I love working out, you big fat slacker. The gym is my life." Well, I am impressed by your workout ethic, and I am so happy you have found a passion for exercise. But finding a balance in your life is important, too. That balance lies somewhere between sitting on the sofa all day long eating bonbons and spending five hours a day at the gym. If your gym time has become your escape hatch from real life, then maybe it's time to cut back a little. Because you'll be in such great shape that you'll probably live for twenty extra years, and that's a lot of extra time to get to have. So make sure, when you go out for a run, that sometimes you run to a bookstore, or to meet a friend; or maybe you could meet a group of friends for a hike, or maybe you could mentor some kid who really needs to get out from behind his computer games and learn how to run a marathon. Keep the balance, and remember to exercise your mind along with your body. But do keep on running, because you're an inspiration to the rest of us.

A FEW WORDS ABOUT EXERCISING FROM SOMEONE WHO KNOWS MORE ABOUT IT THAN I EVER WILL

My friend Katherine is an official two-time Iron Man triath-
lete. Which means that on two different occasions, she took a
2.4-mile swim in the ocean, after which she rode a bike for *112
miles* in raging winds across black lava fields, and then *ran* for *26*
more miles. To be exact, 26.2. That little ".2" might not seem
like a lot to you, but that would probably be the point at which I
would be crawling on bloody knees to the finish line, if I hadn't
already drowned or been eaten by sharks or been blown off my
bicycle into a volcano. This is a woman who runs for 30 miles *just
for fun*. She eats marathons for breakfast. And don't tell her you
"don't have the time" to exercise; she works as a journalist under
hairy, razor-thin deadlines AND raises her two kids as a single
mom, so really, shut up about the "I don't see how I can possibly
squeeze in a half hour of cardio," and the "I'm just not an athlete," and especially the "I know I need to run, but I hate to run."
Her advice about exercise is pretty much this, in a nutshell:

You are an athlete if you want to be. (Say it out loud: "I am
an athlete.") Find the time. Make the time. Don't force yourself
to do something you hate. Make it a part of your life by finding
something you love. If you love to hike, go hiking. If you love
to dance, find a dance class. Make exercise a part of your life-
style, find the joy in it. Start with something you enjoy, and set
goals for yourself. But set manageable goals; you'll set yourself
up for failure if you think you have to spend four hours a day
at the gym, or run five miles every morning. Find partners you
can exercise with, and make it a festive social thing. "Commit to
meeting your partners; if you know they'll be waiting for you at
five thirty A.M. for a run, you have to get yourself out the door
and meet them, or you'll be a bad friend."

Now, isn't that good advice? I admit, I sort of drifted off right around the time I heard "five thirty A.M." and "run," but the rest of it is totally inspiring. And I will just feel like the biggest weenie next time I even think of sleeping in, instead of meeting Ruth and Lisa for a morning constitutional. If Katherine can run through scalding lava fields, I can certainly jog a short mile to the coffeehouse for a latte.

TINA, THE BALLERINA

Maybe you like exercise classes because you prefer it when someone tells you exactly what to do. Maybe you need to have someone behind you with a figurative cattle prod, in order to get yourself in gear. I like classes, in theory, but when I get there I usually find some frantic, shrill, red-faced person shrieking exhortations at the assembled exercisers. The music is set to a level a tiny bit shy of what it takes to make your ears bleed. I just want it to be over as quickly as possible. I know, I should try a nice yoga class, but I think we've got enough people out there doing yoga, don't you? There are only so many downward dogs to go around, after all. You don't need me to swell the ranks. In any event, you can go to any gym and find a fairly good assortment of kickboxing, cardio-salsa, spinning, and aerobic-Pilates-step classes, enough to keep your heart pumping and your eardrums in a permanent state of shock.

A good old-fashioned ballet class is a soothing alternative; but what if you can't find an adult class in your area, and are wary of joining a group of lissome ten-year-olds in pink tights, who have been *tour jeté*–ing since they were toddlers? What if your last encounter with ballet was forty years ago at the Reyna Allen studio and your tutu fell off during your recital? Then *The New York City Ballet Workout* (on DVD) is a wonderful way to get reintroduced. The New York City Ballet dancers aren't delicate *fleurs;* they are powerful, extremely graceful athletes. The workout consists of a pretty classic ballet warm-up, followed by a routine of simple ballet moves. Not too difficult for the beginner, but with room to push yourself if you want to step up the exercise quotient. The music is ballet-class classical, tranquil and elegant, which makes me want to move in a tranquil and elegant manner. It doesn't require a lot of room. Even if you find a few of the moves difficult at first, you can just watch the way the dancers move and move along with them and the nice music. Your steps don't have to be perfect, but I swear, just hanging out with these lovely people will automatically make you stand up a little straighter and carry yourself with a little bit more poise. And when you hold your back straighter, your middle section gets stronger, and then your balance improves. Pretty soon you will start pulling your hair back into a tight chignon and wearing dramatic eyeliner.

And then you can move up to *The New York City Ballet Workout 2,* and you can secretly buy yourself a tutu and reenact the *Swan Lake* death scene in your living room, next time you're home alone.

And maybe a friend of yours will want to join you, and you can both become lean, graceful ballerinas together. *Plié!*

OW. OW.

Okay, so you've gone out there and bounced on your mini-trampoline, and done your little thirty-second sprints, and swung your hula hoop, and jumped with your jump rope. And you discovered that this exercise thing really isn't so bad at all, and you're kind of prancing around feeling all energized and ready to take on your first 5K. And then the next day, you wake up and it dawns on you that you cannot get out of bed. You *can* get out of bed, but you have to use your really sore arms to physically, literally lift your legs off the bed, because your legs won't move on their own without certain muscles that you never knew existed crying out in pain. They are, they're crying out! They're saying, "What in the world have you done to me?" They cannot believe how you have betrayed them. And *you're* thinking, "Hey, whoa, I never even knew you existed, and now you're whining about stuff?" And so on.

Okay, settle down. I don't want to have to separate you two. The thing is, warming up is important, but it turns out that stretching after your workout doesn't really make a difference as to whether or not you'll be sore the next day. It also turns out that it's not all the fault of that mysterious "lactic acid" as we've been told for so many years. It's actually the fault of tiny tears in your muscles; tears that were made when you used those muscles you never knew existed. The tiny tears will make the muscle stronger, but apparently there's no getting around the pain that is caused by the tearing. The sore, cannot-lift-my-leg-up-the-stairs pain will set in a day or two after that workout where you made the acquaintance of those new muscles.

If you are really so sore that you literally cannot lift a cup to your lips, then it would perhaps be best to skip the heavy workout that day. Take a hot bath the evening the soreness sets in. Some people recommend an ice bath, but come *on,* are you serious? An ice bath! That is funny. No, a hot bath actually feels comforting and relaxing, and then you can bundle up in your jammies and crawl into bed right after your bath. My friend Laura, who is also a fantastic massage therapist, highly recommends adding Epsom salts to your bath, pretty much all the time. After your bath, rub arnica gel into the sore spots.

Apparently, it's good to push yourself a little. Apparently, the muscle soreness is a good thing. People who aren't actually experiencing pain will tell you this. The soreness is an indication that the body is being challenged and pushed, and that the muscles are getting stronger. So keep pushing yourself a little bit more every time you work out, but be nice to yourself on the days in between. Take it easy. Which really means, go on a hearty walk, or do something with weights and work on some of those other muscles. Don't work the same group of muscles two days in a row, because you need to give your muscles a day to recover in between workouts. Do squeeze in a walk, because you'll feel better if you move around a little. And stretch. Even if some smarty-pants says it won't help your sore muscles, it just feels good.

In the interest of fairness, and because my friend Geri knows about this stuff, I am forced to tell you that *ice,* not heat, is what is called for, should you have a strain, a sprain, or a nagging pain.

I still think an ice bath sounds just awful.

Geri says you don't need to take an ice bath. She says, just get a little ice pack, and wrap it in a towel, and apply it to the affected area. Leave it on for twenty minutes or so. Take it off for about ten minutes, then back on for another twenty. You can even use a bag of frozen peas, in a pinch. Apparently, the ice pack feels "really good." And I suppose it would feel good, especially knowing that I won't have to climb into a tub of ice water.

REAL-LIFE FITNESS: AMBLING, SAUNTERING, AND MOSEYING

In the not-too-distant past, ladies could throw on a clean housedress, or a neat skirt and sweater set, and—if they were very glamorous—perhaps add a swath of red lipstick and a little powder on the nose. It was enough for an average woman who wasn't Grace Kelly. No one expected them to run five miles, lift some weights, and then build a fabulous gazebo under which they could serve a perfect dinner party for twelve, replete with homegrown baby squashes and tomatoes in aspic. The women who ran five miles and lifted weights were professional athletes, or worked in the circus. If one were naturally the type to throw the dinner party for twelve with the tomato aspic, you wouldn't necessarily catch that same person making her aspic after running the five miles and working out with the weights. The elegant aspic-making type would naturally know her way around a silver tea service, would know how to mix a highball, and if she went outdoors at all, it would only be under the brim of a stylish sun hat, wearing a pair of smart flats. If you did happen to be the hearty, hiking type who enjoyed bracing walks in the country and diving into cold water for fun, you wouldn't necessarily be expected to fool around with aspics, and no one would raise their eyebrows if you didn't have your hair professionally styled. A few bobby pins, strategically placed, and you could call it a day. Now, we are required to be smart, athletic, fashionable, good-looking, sexy, toned, and accomplished, all fine things for which to strive, should one find oneself with a lot of free time. It's not that I pine for those days of foundation garments, basic black and pearls, Aqua Net, and women who don't sweat; even though I adore the cheeky hats and smart ensembles, it's really all for the best. Girdles are ridiculously uncomfortable, and everyone deserves to be able to run around and get sweaty. I mean, in theory. Some of us don't mind moving around, we just find it difficult to stick with a regular program of exercising. We know we're supposed to exercise. Our doctors, or perhaps our thighs have told us so, in no uncertain terms.

But if nothing else, there are ways to make exercising a part of your life, just like we did when we were kids; the same way our mothers and grandmothers used to "exercise." I believe they referred to it as "life." So what you do is simply this: instead of always driving those three blocks to the drugstore or coffee-house, walk, on those lovely strong legs of yours. Walk if you can, whenever you can. Slow down your life just a little and walk, walk, walk. Instead of taking an hour out of your day to walk on a treadmill and lift weights, walk or ride your bike to do short errands. Take the stairs instead of an elevator. Take the stairs two at a time instead of the escalator. Get your workouts when you can find them, make movement fit into each day. Do squats or lunges while you're watching the news, or waiting for your tea water to boil. Jump up and down in place while you're waiting for the coffee to be ready, or talking to your husband. He'll get used to it. Do calf raises in the shower, or while brushing your teeth. Do push-ups against the kitchen counter while you're making breakfast. Meet friends for a walk instead of meeting for drinks. While you're sitting at your desk or in the car, tense your abdominal muscles, pulling your belly button back toward your spine for twenty seconds, working up to several repetitions every other morning. Alternate with sets of Kegel exercises: contract and release your pelvic floor muscles. Every time you go into the office kitchen, do thirty jumping jacks. Every time you glance at the clock, do some shoulder and neck rolls. Jog in place for sixty seconds, drop and do ten push-ups; do lunges as you walk. Putter in your garden, or in the park. Lift a child (perhaps yours?) into the air. Larger children can go on a walk with you, or you can run a few races with them, to get some short sprints in. Find various destinations one to three miles from your house and make weekend walking excursions out of visiting those destinations. Pretty soon it will feel weird to get in the elevator instead of taking the stairs. Pretty soon, getting into the car to drive three blocks will just feel silly, so you'll walk. And pretty soon you'll start feeling more fit and energized. Your energy will be infectious, and friends will get out of their cars and start walking more, and pretty soon the air will be cleaner and neighbors will meet neighbors, and the world will be a veritable utopia. Wow. That was easy.

YOUR MIDLIFE FASHION CRISIS:
NOW WHAT?

MAGAZINES AND MAKEOVER SHOWS ARE HAPPY TO TELL US what to wear and what not to wear when we're in our forties and fifties. "Do" wear a subtle shade of beige or ecru, "do" wear a tasteful pulled-together ensemble, like this sophisticated sweater set and understated tan slacks. "Do" tone down your makeup, and whatever you do, "don't" dress too "young." The tasteful ensembles they suggest are lovely, inoffensive, and, er . . . tasteful. Which is fine, if your taste runs to tasteful ensembles. But what if you're the type of woman who has always loved the fun of fashion? Where's the fun in a pale pink cardigan? I have always admired an ecru Armani pantsuit, and the willowy women who wear that sort of thing. But some of us are under, say, six feet tall; certain items of clothing just do not look the same on us as they do on a lanky model with coat-hanger shoulders and a lean torso.

If we like fashion, we've managed to devise a style for ourselves that attempts to take into account the fact that we don't necessarily possess a conventional amount of conventional beauty; a style that takes into account our interesting body type and our height. But then our bodies start changing a little, and we start second-guessing our fashion choices, and suddenly we feel disconnected from all those things we used to love about dressing up.

And so here we are, on the precipice of a new era, hurling headlong into midlife. Suddenly many of us are becoming very timid about fashion, for fear of inappropriately not "dressing our age." We've always loved kicky vintage clothing, but now we wonder if that 1930s housedress will just make us look like we're understudying Ma Joad in a *Grapes of Wrath* dinner theater production. Some of us have neither the inclination nor the financial wherewithal to pop into Prada or pay a visit to Mr. Dolce & Mr. Gabbana's little shop so that we can feel stylish and confident in our fashion choices; so, to be on the safe side, we start dressing more carefully and conventionally. But why should "dressing our age" automatically mean dressing more conservatively? How can we reinvent our sense of style but remain true to our authentic selves?

When we reach a certain age, we sometimes feel as if we've "disappeared." We may feel invisible. We feel that we no longer inspire poetry, or feverish love letters. We fear that men are no longer inclined to walk into walls or into oncoming traffic after glancing into our mysterious eyes, or watching our retreating figure as we spring down the street in our strappy sandals. Perhaps they never did any of those things, but we feel they may have been a lot closer to walking into walls then than they are now.

Well, I think that this should give us greater freedom to be adventurous in our fashion choices. It should be a reason to avoid the beige pantsuit, not a reason to wear the beige pantsuit. We don't have to be invisible to ourselves. We don't need to give in to the beige pantsuit. Do not succumb to the beige pantsuit!

Of course, many of you feel perfectly comfortable in your boxy, elastic-waist, gauzy ensembles, specifically designed for the middle-aged gal. Leave me alone, you're thinking. Where do you get off telling me not to wear my sweatshirt with the funny cats on it? And just because you don't like my taupe sweater tunic and viscose-blend slacks doesn't mean I shouldn't wear them. I don't want to wear a little black dress, and you're an idiot.

You, of course, have special dispensation from these fashion suggestions, because you are confident and happy with your fashion taste. Whatever you have going on, it is working for you. Perhaps you look particularly fetching in a beige pantsuit, and have really cemented your beige pantsuit "look." But if you're one of those women who are unhappy or frustrated by your current personal style or lack thereof—or, if you wear overalls—then you might want to give yourself a little fashion therapy. In some cases, electroshock fashion therapy.

We're real grown-up women now, and we don't have to blend into the background in our tasteful yet casual ensembles. I think we've earned the right to dress ourselves up without worrying whether or not we're "age-appropriate." Dress to your best advantage rather than jump from trend to trend. Let's blaze this trail together, ladies. Let's show the world what an exciting, excited, creative, active, and confident grown-up looks like.

At the grocery store, at the dentist, there are always a couple of female celebrities staring up at us from a magazine cover, who look as if they've been crammed into their gowns with a shoehorn. They're "Over Forty and Fabulous!" or "Fifty and Fantastic!" And their dresses are all "Sexy" and "HOT!!"—not because the dresses are particularly attractive, but because the copywriters had to do something to deflect from the desperate look of forced gaiety on the faces of the fabulously sexy middle-aged ladies. I don't know if there is anything more uncomfortable-looking than someone who has been told to seduce the camera.

The headlines imply that with a little willpower and hard work, I, too, could be that fabulous, and I think to myself, "Do I have to be?" Of course I want to be fabulous, who doesn't want to be fabulous? But do I have to stuff myself into some body-hugging, hideous-looking designer outfit, jam my feet into high heels, and keep myself in a constant state of semi-starvation? Do I really want to achieve that slightly puffy and vaguely simian fat-injected face, the aggressively toned abdominal muscles, that crazy look of triumph over nature?

So here you are, over forty, or fifty, but you don't look fabulous in *that* way. Nor do you know if you really want to look fabulous in that way. It looks vaguely constricting. It looks like a lot of work. A *lot*.

I think you're already quite fabulous. But fabulous has nothing to do with whittling yourself down to a size 0 and never eating spaghetti again in your life. Fabulous has even less to do with the fact that you have somehow—through surgery, injectables, or a relentless schedule of laser treatments and spray tint—managed to make yourself look like a tanned and healthy twenty-five-year-old.

I look at pictures of myself when I was twenty-five, and I am kinda cute, even if I was woefully unaware of how cute I was.

But I was a completely different person. I have a photograph of myself taken by a boyfriend of mine, when I was about twenty-four. I'm wearing some strapless satin-y blue dress with a ruffled skirt. Ruffles! I don't really like ruffles, and I hate that shade of blue. And yet there I am! A completely different person. And then there I am again, with a feather in my braided hair, and an embroidered fringed shawl. And again, with platinum-blond hair and an oversize man's shirt. Leg warmers! That vintage dress with the smocking. That weird haircut that looked like some tragic cross between Louise Brooks and Keely Smith.

Sadly, there is no photographic evidence of me wearing a red petticoat on my head, which I liked to do quite often because it was a good stand-in for long, red, princess hair. I wore tights on my head too, as a medieval princess headdress. Also, I wore underpants on my head. With my hair pulled out the leg holes. So many fashion statements, so little time.

But all of the dizzying array of costumes and headdresses and hairdos made me realize that we all get to have—very much like cats—something like nine lives. Maybe more. Our faces change, they mutate and shift. Our bodies alter, add, subtract, adjust, adapt. We try underpants on our heads (surely it wasn't just me), along with berets, cowboy hats, bandannas, wedding veils, straw sun hats, and an adorable vintage leopard pillbox. We've done whatever we did at twenty-five, and then we did something else at thirty-two. It's time to move on. We get to reinvent ourselves a few more times. And no matter what direction we take, fashion is a delightful way to express ourselves and to present ourselves to the world.

On the other hand, you don't always feel like expressing

yourself every minute of the day, or going to a lot of trouble making a presentation of yourself to the world. Sometimes you just want to be comfortable, or cozy, warm or cool, depending on the season. Sometimes you just want to throw on an old sweater and a pair of worn-in jeans. So of course you should feel comfortable enough to wear your nap-on-the-sofa attire, too.

As we age, yes . . . less, less is more. Most of the time. Less is more, except when it is definitely not. As we swim in the waters of the fabulous Over Forties, perhaps we need to balance Less Is More with I Feel I Need A Long Chiffon Scarf With This Outfit. You have earned the right to carry a little more panache and aplomb. You have earned your dramatic hat, your artful lip and eyebrow. You've also earned the right to go out into the world fresh-faced and completely bereft of all makeup, if that is how you feel best. (Just don't forget the sunblock.) Remember, fashion can be pricey, but style is free!

GROOMING SHORTCUTS!
HOW CAN I DO LESS?
(And Still Be Able to Leave the House without Getting Arrested for Vagrancy)

> *When I got ready for New Year's Eve in four minutes, from "nursing mommy wear" to glittery black dress, stockings, high heels, my longtime guy friend was waiting for me, noted my then-husband's indifference to the speed of transformation, and said, "He doesn't know what he's got."*
> —LESLIE, ON HER FAVORITE COMPLIMENT

> *Before he became my husband, Fredo said I was his kind of woman because I woke up beautiful, didn't need or use any makeup, and only took five minutes to get dressed no matter where I was heading.*
> —DIANA, ON HER FAVORITE COMPLIMENT

GETTING YOURSELF DRESSED AND OUT OF THE HOUSE WITHOUT necessarily looking as if you spent the night under the freeway overpass can sometimes be a feat. Time can be an issue. Especially for mothers of young children. And for mothers of older children. Also for women who work. And for women who don't work. And for women who are over forty, and women who are over fifty, and for women who have to be somewhere and can't find their glasses so that they can read the label on the back of the bottle. Is it hand cream or shampoo? I can't tell if that's a lip pencil or an eyeliner pencil. Oh. It's an eyeliner pencil. I have black lips. Crap. Where is my other shoe?

The bar keeps moving higher and higher for basic body and facial maintenance, seeming to reach impossible heights the older we get. Getting out of the house in five minutes flat just isn't the breeze it once was. It's enough to make you stay in your pajamas all day long, if by "pajamas" I really mean "old shirt inherited from teenage son, paired with cut-off sweatpants."

For many women, it's easier than ever before to get out of the house in five minutes flat. We no longer need to impress every person in our airspace. For that matter, we no longer care if we impress anyone at all. As many of us age, we simply can't be bothered about what everyone thinks of us. We just don't give a damn. But this doesn't mean we should just give up completely and start wearing sweatshirts with teddy bear appliqués and cute sayings on them. We don't want to forget that we're wearing a gravy-stained poncho and a pair of Hello Kitty slippers when we trot off to the store for a loaf of bread.

Here are my tools for pulling yourself together in a very, very short amount of time. Can I promise that you will be able to Pull Yourself Together in Five or Ten Minutes? That all depends on how fast you can move. But I can pretty much guarantee you'll be ready in No Time Flat if you follow these quick beauty tips:

Get yourself a nice **foundation stick** that matches your skin tone. Bobbi Brown is my favorite. As we get older, the point is to use as little foundation as possible (because of the unfortunate way it has of settling into the crevices, as I mentioned). So, after cleansing and moisturizing, take your nice stick foundation and swipe it on those few areas you think might benefit from a little evening out. Might I suggest a swipe on either side of your nose and one swipe on each lower corner of your mouth? Then, with your finger, lightly blend out and up.

My best secret for your eyes: Lancôme **black kohl pencil**, inside the rim of the eyes. Blink a few times, then take a Q-tip and neaten the corners. Or don't neaten the corners, for the look that says, "I am a French movie star and I just rolled out of bed. I know it's noon, shut up. Where is my champagne?"

Eyebrows. Those skinny MAC eyebrow pencils are indispensable for shaping, as well as the Maybelline Define-a-Brow— with the cute little built-in comb—for a less expensive alternative. Also, brush your eyebrows up and trim them along the top, if those long curly grandpa hairs start showing up.

Eyeliner. When I use it, I like liquid or gel. MAC or Bobbi Brown. But my friend Bella, who's the eyeliner expert, just showed me a new one she found from Clarins. It's sort of an eyeliner pen, and when you shake it, the tiny brush fills up with eyeliner ink and makes a really nice line without you having to possess the skills of a master painter.

Loose powder in translucent or with a little pigment (I like Bobbi Brown yellow #1), which will blot away the oily spots without making you look as if you've started production on the remake of *Whatever Happened to Baby Jane?* Use a cotton ball to apply—but just on your forehead, on and around your nose, your chin, and wherever you don't want your face to look shiny.

But you want to keep a few shiny spots, like on your cheeks; if a little shine pokes through the powder, then it will look much more natural.

If nothing else, a **perfect red lipstick.** Happy hunting! Might I direct you to my favorite purveyors of lipstick? Most cosmetic lines offer a fine assortment of lipsticks, but for reasons beyond my comprehension none of them is particularly weighted toward really good reds. MAC may be the exception. And one of the best reds ever is made by a makeup artist named Julie Hewitt. Coco Noir, a red to send other reds slinking away in burning shame. Gorgeous color, matte but not too dry, old Hollywood glamour, impossible to get your hands on (but try her Web site, www .juliehewitt.net). As far as the more easily accessible brands, the least I can do is share my many years of tireless research and testing of various reds. The following run the gamut from bright reds to deep purple-y reds. Mix and match. Collect 'em all!

MAC: Dubonnet, X-treme, Ruby Woo, Viva Glam, Media, Miss Dish, Retro

Nars: Fire Down Below, Red Lizard, Shanghai Red, Scarlet Empress, and my new favorite, the Velvet Matte lip pencil in "Cruella." Swoony!

Clinique: Vintage Wine

Julie Hewitt: Coco Noir, Femme Noir

Chanel: Vamp, Russet Moon

Bobbi Brown: Burnt Red

Use alone, or try layering a few. Don't be afraid to try different combinations until you get exactly the right, most flattering shade of red. (For instance, try Ruby Woo with a layer of Dubonnet on top. Mr. DeMille, I'm ready for my close-up! I'm just saying.)

Also a **pashmina shawl** is often the very thing needed to get you out of the house with the least amount of fuss.

"Hang on a minute," you say. "A little while back, you declared shawls to be horrible. What gives, lady?" Okay, here's the deal with shawls. Shawls are sometimes used by women attempting to disguise a large midsection, or camouflage Jell-O batwings. They have gotten a bad rap because of that, but shawls are not just for hiding behind when you're feeling fat. They can also be dashing and dramatic, and, need we mention, er, warm. The perfect accessory when a little chill has set in and you don't want to wear a bulky down parka. Also, let's just spit it out here: some of us do need a little, shall we say, veiling over our upper arms. And a shawl is the perfect way to keep the chill off while showing a little shoulder but also conveniently shrouding the upper arms in a way that doesn't look as if you're hiding under a tent. A black shawl can look very elegant and Felliniesque with the right kind of pulled-back hair, strong eyebrows, and dangling earrings, but it can also look a little Old Country if your hair is hanging down in drab clumps and you've got on some lackluster, nondescript number. You don't want to look like a Sicilian Mafia grandmother in mourning. A shawl is actually the perfect accessory to perk up a lackluster, nondescript number, but if it's a black shawl, you'll have to go that extra mile to perk it up, whether with a hat, jewelry, or a swath of bright lipstick. Unless you are totally into the Sicilian Mafia grandmother look. That could work. Seriously, you can pull it off.

I used to have the most perfect Japanese-designed **black overcoat.** But it wasn't a big, weighty thing; it wasn't the kind of coat that was meant to ward off serious weather. It was light, unlined, and beautifully made of the most delicate wool gabardine. It hung in a lovely, drape-y way. You could be wearing striped pajamas under it, and you would look as if you were ready to go have martinis at the Plaza. It could dress up just about anything. So you can imagine, if you have a coat like this, and you don't have time for your normal morning routine, all you need to do is pull your hair back in a sleek ponytail, slap on a little red lipstick, and you're ready to face the world. The coat shouldn't be too heavy, though. Suit-weight, or dress-weight. Nice and light. Simple. Elegantly designed. And if you find one, please tell me where I can get another, because mine was stolen.

Hair. Sometimes a loosely pinned, slightly messy twisted bun or ponytail looks better with very elegant clothing than a sleek, perfectly coiffed chignon. If your makeup and clothing are polished and pulled together, a slightly untidy head makes a nice contrast, as if you were busy living your fabulous life, stopped for a few minutes to pull on your superb dress and give yourself a swath of lipstick, and, as an afterthought, pulled your hair back with your fingers. Conversely, a very sleek hairdo will pull together any old baggy cardigan-and-khaki combo, for those days when it's all you can do to throw on the first thing you grab in the morning.

Of course, all the fabulous beauty tips in the world won't work at all unless you get lots of sleep, eat well, and live a good life. You know this. But it's really true, about the smiling. You can slather on the thousand-dollar face cream, you can have

YOU LOOK FINE, REALLY

your face cut and sculpted by the finest surgeon in the kingdom, but if you're a crabby old jerk, people still won't want to hang out with you. So think nice thoughts and don't be bitter and cranky, because it will show up in your face. Coco Chanel's little saying about "getting the face you deserve by the time you turn fifty" isn't about laugh lines and those little furrows that come from thinking about things.

Though it may seem as if we're speeding past our expiration date, it's really all a matter of perception. Perhaps we used to be more *jolie,* but honestly, it's much more interesting to be *jolie-laide.* In our twenties, heads might've snapped as we walked down the street, but now our demographic has changed. Our target audience has evolved. And even though we no longer may give as much of a hoot, it's important to give at least a small hoot. Make the effort for yourself, because it's fun. And make a dazzling effort for your inner circle, because it'll put the bubbles in everyone's champagne and make you feel like a million. Dollars, that is.

ACCENTUATE YOUR POSITIVES
HERE IS A STORY ABOUT A DRESS

So I WENT TO THIS FABULOUS DRESS SHOP HERE IN LOS ANGELES. I hardly ever go out to fabulous dress shops, because I am usually afraid of going into them, because they scare me. They scare me because everything inside is so beautiful and gleaming with possibility, and I assume that I cannot afford to buy anything in the fabulous store, so therefore I don't even want to step inside. My inner demons are telling me that the minute I walk into the fabulous store, the salesperson will recognize me for the fraudulent shopper that I am. She will see my shabby coat, or my short stature, or some mark on my forehead visible only to dress shop managers and salespeople, and know immediately that I do not belong there. She will take one glance at my nose, or my handbag, or my shoes, and she'll know that I have no business looking through the racks or ogling the accessories.

But I was with my good friend Wendy, so hanging firmly on her coattails, I entered this cathedral of clothing, this ode to adorable adornment. I am a sucker for a sweet frock, I live for finding the perfect frock, and so I entered, and my pulse quickened, and I was in frock heaven.

Then I found this dress. It was, in so many ways, the perfect dress. It was black, and fell very low on the shoulders. It was voluminous, with these weird, long sashes attached to the front, which the designer meant to be wrapped around the body in a mummy-like fashion and tied in front. Or back. In a bow. Or a knot. I loved the fabric, I loved the idea of the dress, it was . . . unusual. I just wasn't sure about the mummy wrapping. I wasn't sure I was completely on board with the designer's intent. But I tried on the dress, and I tied it up like a mummy, and the sales-girl went "Ooh!" and the shop owner went "Aah!" and my friend Wendy declared the frock to be stunning and flattering. It didn't quite feel right. I untied the mummy wrapping and let the long sashes drop down and let the dress be all voluminous, and everyone squinted and looked, and made "tsk-tsk" faces, and said I really shouldn't be afraid to show my curves, and that the sashes were really meant to wrap the dress up like a mummy, and that wearing it all loose and voluminous just made it look like a *nightgown*.

The price was certainly too high for a voluminous black nightgown, and even too high for a dress that I might have absolutely adored. But the pressure was insidious, and the dress suddenly represented the complicated mash-up of feelings roiling around inside: if I don't buy it, I'm admitting that I can't really afford it, that I don't deserve to buy a fun, expensive dress, that the cost of this dress really represents five normal dresses for me, who doesn't deserve to be here in the first place. But if I bought those five normal dresses instead, they would be conventional, and boring, and would serve only to cover my body and provide a modicum of comfort and style. If I buy this sweet, voluminous black frock, I'm allowing myself possibility. Panache. An unknown quantity of whatever it is that allows a certain type of woman to pop off to the frock shop and pull a pretty thing off the rack and buy it, without fretting for three hours. I'm further- ing the unique expression of my inner creative girly girl.

Let me just say: this is a lot of baggage to carry when pur- chasing a dress.

I bought the dress. And I got it home, and tried it ten dif- ferent ways to Sunday. I stood in front of the mirror and tried it with the mummy wrapping, and the tying, and a big bow and a little bow; I wrapped it Empire-style, below the waist, and at the waist. It was a disaster. "Buyer's remorse" doesn't even begin to describe the utter folly of what I had done. I sadly, gently, hung the voluminous black dress on a hanger and put it in my closet.

Months, months later, I had forgotten all about the volumi- nous black dress. Too embarrassed to return it, as if that would declare to the stylish shop and the world that I had no idea how to wear a really special creation such as this black dress, it hung in my closet as a reminder that I was too extravagant, and unde- serving of my extravagant nature. But then I had a party coming up, and nothing to wear to the party, and I thought about the black dress. I pulled it out, and I put it on. Backward.

Backward, the shoulders of the dress fell romantically off the edge of my shoulders, and the long sashes fell behind me in a long train. I tied the long, long sashes into a giant bow behind me, and the sash ends trailed in a modified train. The weight of the sashes kept the dress sitting just so—under my collarbone in front, leaving my back bare and open, with a big, droopy bow at my tailbone. The dress was suddenly ethereal and gossamer, and I didn't feel as if I was wearing a nightgown at all. Especially since there was nobody there to tell me that it looked like one. Suddenly, I loved that black dress. I was so happy I'd bought it. It's exactly the frock I wanted. It's the sweetest frock. With sparkly earrings and a pair of gold sandals, it's a frock fit for a fairy princess. With a pair of flip-flops and a sun hat, it's a summer afternoon party frock, fit for a latent California girl who is a fairy princess in her head.

Figure out what your best assets are, if you haven't already done it, and accentuate them. If you don't have a large bust but you've got a pretty collarbone, wear lower-cut and off-the-shoulder clothing. If you love your bust but not your neck or arms, a tight black turtleneck might be just the ticket. If you're a happy fireplug of a person, with a short waist and neck, don't let anyone talk you into anything with padded shoulders and a voluminous gathered skirt. You can update items in your closet with a few simple makeovers. Shorten jacket and coat sleeves to make bracelet or three-quarter-length sleeves. Cut off your pants to make summer capris; if you have some dresses in your closet that you think don't work anymore, then give them away, give them to friends; but before you do, try them on one more time. Backward.

GLOVES, PARASOLS, FANS, AND HANKIES

For various reasons, I believe that certain anachronistic accoutrements from bygone days should be brought back into our lives. Not just for style purposes but because they're totally practical. You may think gloves and a parasol the height of frivolity, but, in fact, both accessories could be your secret weapon in skin care. Yes, we should be wearing some kind of sunblock every day. And although sunscreen is now available that doesn't make the wearer look like a kabuki ghost, it is suddenly being discovered that many of those nice, modern lightweight sunscreens are full of carcinogens (oxybenzone, methylparaben), and wearing them may be worse than wearing no sunscreen at all. Much, much worse.

Okay, but now what? I say, let's take our cue from the centuries of women who knew to protect their own skin with gloves and a parasol. Yes, it may be impractical and uncomfortable to wear high-necked blouses, long sleeves, and veils, but gloves and a parasol are two easy accessories that will keep the sun off while simultaneously giving you a fabulous *je ne sais quoi*. In warm weather, they will keep your hands, face, and neck protected from the sun; in the fall and winter they will protect you from cold and inclement weather. Added bonus? I met a fabulous lady once, at a holiday cocktail party. She wore a lovely pair of gloves throughout the party (although I believe she took them off to eat) and when I asked about them, she revealed that she wears gloves for the entire holiday season, and she never gets the flu.

As for fans and hankies, these may be the most practical accessories of all, for those awkward times when you are suddenly overcome by sweaty, drenching hot flashes. Far better than sitting frozen with a horrified look on your face while rivulets of perspiration begin dripping off the end of your nose is languidly fanning yourself with a pretty fan and simultaneously dabbing at your dewy upper lip. The discomfort and panic will immediately subside; your embarrassing dampness will be instantly fanned away, to be replaced by a dash of chic.

Sun damage, flu, and hot flashes may all be facts of life, but we can make them minor annoyances to be faced head-on with panache and a few good props.

CURLY TOP, YOU LITTLE BUNDLE OF JOY

I just wonder about my curly-headed friends sometimes. I just do. They don't seem to understand what they've got on their heads. And when I hear of the trials they undergo in order to procure straight hair, I genuinely don't get it. I would like to tell them to just embrace their frizz, thereby giving themselves extra, untold hours every morning. I would like to appeal to their practical sense of time usage and efficiency. To point out that a few hours of extra beauty sleep will do more for them than a blowout. But alas, spending two hours blowing their hair straight has become just part of the morning routine.

If I told you that you could save a few extra hours in the morning *and* not end up looking like a Beverly Hills matron, that would be mean of me; but wouldn't it sound like a deal? Even though you think straight hair is the most beautiful, unattainable crowning glory you could possibly ever want, straight hair is not necessarily flattering on every face. In short, you have been looking at too many sleek-headed nineteen-year-old waifs in magazines. Okay, admittedly, I have stick-straight hair. Anemic baby-fine hair, thin and flat. I have longed for glossy ringlets my whole life. I'd even settle for a pile of frizz, which my wavy-headed friends tell me is only a curse, an unholy mess that must be battled and tamed into submission. But I am telling you, your curls are so beautiful. They suit you. They frame your face in a cloud of billowing waywardness. If you're a hat person, you will understand when I say that, to me, having curls is like getting to wake up in the most fabulous furry hat. A hat you can sleep in! I imagine being able to wake up, roll out of bed, and without even having to bother with the application of lipstick and powder, my visage is framed in a ready-made bonnet of pre-Raphaelite beauty.

How can I impart to you, my wavy-, frizzy-, curly-, twisty-, bouncy-haired friends, your amazing luck at winning the hair lotto? How can I tell you that you look much prettier with that enviable pile of hairy unruliness on your head? It gives you instant Bohemian credentials; it gives you the look of having been kept in bed past the alarm due to sweaty sex. It implies a head full of passion and ferocity. You can still cinch it back in a neat little bun so that when you do let it loose, a gentleman might be inclined to swallow hard and say, "Why, Miss Brown, I've never seen you with your hair down," as his neck turns a beet-ish shade of red. With a wild head of curls, you can also wear the sleekest, plainest outfit, and you've got an instant accessory. All hail the curly head!

Note to my straight-haired readers: I don't mean to make you feel bad with all that rah-rah stuff and fawning over the curly-headed people, but honestly, they are so insecure about their hair! So you have to be really, really nice to them, and constantly tell them how horrible and stringy your own straight hair is.

Nothing against straight hair, really. I mean, it's all over my head. I've grown used to it, and have found things to love about it. It doesn't have the fabulous hat-like qualities of a head of curly hair, but it has its own appeal. After all, why would curly-headed people pay thousands of dollars to have their hair coated in chemicals so they can have it too? I mean, let's be appreciative of the sleek shininess of it! Flip it, swing it, enjoy the fact that when you wake up in the morning you look relatively unlike a lunatic who has run through a windstorm. (And for you curly-headed types who are still reading, who tell me that when you wake up in the morning you *do* look very much like a lunatic who has run through a windstorm, I was only kidding about that last part. Straight hair, ugh! Puh-leez. Nothing to write home about, believe me. No instant hat in the morning at *all*, just the same ol' same ol' mousy strands of flatness. Honestly. Curls are the *best*.)

Perhaps it's time to stop the madness. Perhaps it's time to take a deep breath and accept your perceived flaws. Why not try this: wake up tomorrow morning and look in the mirror. Look with your critical eyes at your poochy belly, or your stick-straight hair, or your sparse eyelashes, or the little bulb on the end of your nose. Look at your poochy belly, and then feel how you're going to feel going through the rest of your life hating that part of yourself. I mean really. The rest of your life. Hating your nose, your hair, your ankles, your belly. Then just decide to accept the way it is, for one whole, entire day. Just love it. For one whole day. Look at that poochy belly and remind yourself that this is your belly, and it's part of your remarkable body, which is the only body you get to have in this lifetime. And if you can love it for that one whole day, then maybe you can love it for the next whole day. Maybe you won't love it every day, but you can just take it one day at a time and see how it goes. And maybe if you get more in the habit of loving those little parts of yourself that you're in the habit of hating, then maybe the love part will start outweighing the hate part, and the hate part will start seeming a little silly. Because, I mean, you *hate* your hair? *Hating* your hair is really worth all that energy?

If you're lucky enough to be in love with someone who loves you back and gives you lots of COMPLIMENTS, make sure you listen, really listen, and really take them in, you lucky duck.

Sometimes compliments are NOT really meant as compliments, but end up being. One of the best compliments I have ever received:

Christie, you look like a stolen car.
——Ross Graham

Thank you, Ross!

"I was in Belgrade, Serbia, city of ass-pants and blowouts
and boob jobs and super-iridescent, shiny, holographic disco
makeup. A woman at my table said, "Joo are so strange, so
. . . so . . . MEEnimal!"

——My friend Alexandra Oliver,
on her favorite compliment

"Only an artist could put that outfit together and pull it off."
—My friend Ruth Souza's favorite compliment

FUZZY GLASSES AND OTHER ACCESSORIES

In this brave new world of super high-definition digital television, when the very pores on the faces of glamorous people suddenly appear to be veritable craters, one longs for the days of soft focus and pink lighting. The real world is harsh enough, and as we age, wouldn't it be nice to have a little soft focus now and again? Of course I adore those little crinkles in the corners of my eyes. I've earned those delightful little laugh lines. I did not, however, earn those lines that seem to be forming around the sides of my mouth, no idea where they came from. I did not earn, nor do I want those jowly things that are starting up along my jawline. So on those days when we feel more jowly than crinkly, one thing you might try is to make gifts of fuzzy glasses to your friends.

Fuzzy glasses are custom-treated lenses formulated to cause the wearer to see your face in soft, fuzzy focus. They're easy to make at home, and can be given to friends, coworkers, dates, and fellow partygoers. With a small outlay of cash and a simple assembly line, you can make a boxful of fuzzy glasses that may be passed out at dinner parties, luncheons, blind dates, or in social situations where you suspect the lighting may be less than flattering. Simply take a pair of clear, nonprescription glasses and an old nylon stocking. Stretch the stocking over the frames, making cuts for the eyeglass arms to poke through. In a pinch, Instant Fuzzy Glasses may be fashioned with the easy application of Vaseline or lip balm directly onto the lenses. Voilà! You will now appear to be the beautiful, slightly blurry version of that woman of mystery you know yourself to be.

Problems may arise when you encounter a less-than-cooperative friend or dinner companion. "I'm not putting on those stupid glasses," they might say, or "What the hell is smeared all over the lenses?" And there you are, in all that harsh lighting, feeling distinctly un-fuzzy and in full, sharp focus. So what happens when your friends just simply refuse to wear the fuzzy glasses? How are we to put ourselves into soft focus without spending the three hours that may be required in front of the vanity, once we become transfixed by the horrors seen in the magnifying mirror?

It may be time to pull out the big guns. Veils! Let's bring back the veil. I'm not talking about a chador, or some kind of burka-like contraption. I mean the kind of veil popularized in the 1930s and 1940s. The kind that was usually attached to a sloping brim of a fetching cloche or hat of some kind, the kind from which you'd peek out in an enigmatic and/or coy manner. Veils can be a simple mesh-like affair, or they can sport dots and sequins to add a whimsical note to your air of mystery. There is no one who doesn't look fabulous with a little black netting over her face, and very few people who look terible in a hat.

And speaking of hats: just for fun, think about the idea of wearing a hat, not just to keep the sun off your face (although that's being smart and stylish) but because it's chic and sort of silly. Wear a hat to pull your outfit together: a beret with your trench or peacoat, a crushable fedora in the spring, a chunky knit cap in the fall. Pop on a cute bucket hat when you're having a bad hair day, or just to add a dollop of whimsy to your ensemble. And pretty soon, maybe more hats will start appearing, and then powder compacts, and red lipstick and cocktail rings. And what could be wrong with adding a little more style to the world?

VINTAGE? WHY NOT?

Some of us lived in vintage clothing in our formative years, and well beyond, in some cases. But now, with these birthdays really piling on, we fear that wearing vintage clothing might make us look as if we're wearing a costume, or like the bag lady we've always secretly feared we'd become. But there is no need for you to give up something you love, if you really love it. If you can find vintage pieces that fit well, then wear them with pride, knowing that everyone was a lot smaller back then. Yay, you and your eighteen-inch waist! But if you keep trying on that 1940s silk housedress over and over, and it's pooching out in places it never used to pooch out—or you somehow are looking less like Rita Hayworth and more like your great-aunt Pearl, then perhaps it's time to reassess your vintage look. Dowdy is kind of adorable when you're twenty-two. Perhaps not so much a few decades later.

Vintage accessories are a great way to spike your wardrobe; without looking as if you're heading to a theme party, you can add interest to an ordinary outfit: a handbag here, a scarf there. Maybe just the jacket from a vintage women's suit, coupled with a pair of modern slim pants; or a unique hat to wear with a contemporary sundress. I have a camel cashmere blanket coat I got at a vintage store years ago for $15. (Sorry, don't mean to rub it in. Yes, it's gorgeous.) It's a big coat, and it can easily overwhelm whatever it's on top of and just be too much. But it's so warm and cozy, and feels like a big blanket, so I try to balance it with something simple and slim underneath. You can even pull together that cute baggy 1940s housedress you've always loved so much; cinch it with a shiny new belt, or pair it with a short black cardigan. Funky is still fun, and it's still very satisfying for some of us to mix up great old unmatched pieces that we love, and call it our Sunday best. And I don't see why the fun should end now.

> ## NOTE ON SHOPPING:
> NO, IT'S NOT A REAL HOBBY

ESSENTIAL LUXURIES

Every woman needs a few essential luxuries, even when doing a little belt-tightening. Obviously, an "essential luxury" is going to have a different meaning from one person to the next. To you, an essential luxury might mean that great haircut, because it enables you to get out of the house in five minutes. Perhaps you've never been a manicure person, but now suddenly you've decided that a manicure once a week is a necessary treat and makes you feel all glossy and spiffed up, no matter what you're wearing. We want the best results for the least effort, at this age, and I appreciate anything that helps me pull myself together without having to fuss for an hour in front of a mirror. A good hair clip. An elegant coat. A stylish pair of reading glasses. For you it might be a well-made bra that fits perfectly, or a monthly trip to the hair salon for ashy highlights, or a Swiss Army knife, or a beautiful silk nightgown, or a really cute bike.

Dress for the boys, or dress for the girls, but mostly dress for yourself. If you're not that into you, you should be.

YES, YOU'RE A VITAL, GORGEOUS WOMAN WHO CAN WEAR ANYTHING YOU FEEL LIKE WEARING! EXCEPT THAT. DO NOT. WEAR. THAT. (JUST . . . DO NOT WEAR IT, I BEG OF YOU.)

Um, how do I put this . . . that skirt? Well, when you're nineteen and you've got those coltish legs sticking out the bottom, or possibly some very supportive undergarments, I think that skirt might not look quite so much like you forgot to get dressed. And when you have reached your elegant golden years, perhaps the backless terry-cloth hot-pants ensemble does not show your graceful self to the best advantage. I know, I know, from the back you look like a teenager. But from the front, you really don't. Because you aren't, in fact, a teenager; you are a lovely older woman inexplicably stuffed inside a hot-pink skintight Lycra tube dress. Of course, your body is a beautiful thing, no matter what shape or size. But perhaps others may not want to see quite so much of it, outside of a swimming pool or beach or nudist camp.

Also, I want to be nice about this, but . . . did you step on a Yeti? I mean, those boots. Those boots that look as if they're eating your feet. I guess I always thought the fur was supposed to go on the inside of the boot. You know, to keep your toes nice and toasty. And when they put it on the outside like that, well, it looks like you've got a couple of Lhasa apsos tied to your feet. Also, you might rethink the one-shouldered Grecian toga minidress. I know it looked really, really good when you saw it on the pages of *Vogue,* but don't forget the lady wearing it is eighteen years old and has no discernible midsection. Also, her legs are six feet long. And she is paid large quantities of money to be naturally beautiful. You'd think that sort of thing wouldn't matter, but it really does when it comes to one-shouldered mini-dresses.

That doesn't mean we can't have fun, and of course we can embrace our own unique shapes and curves and loveliness. But aesthetics are also a good thing to embrace. And dignity. And perhaps a tiny air of mystery. And a smidgen of good taste. Those are all things that are nice to have as we enter our exciting later years.

Many rules are just asking to be broken, so of course you should make your own decisions regarding the white leather shorts, the butt-length blond hair extensions, and the baby-doll minidress. Perhaps they suit you to a T.

Right here is where I'd say, "You go, girl!" but I absolutely hate it when people say that. Honestly, please don't say it any-more. Let's just retire it, along with "twenty-four-seven," "at the end of the day," and "kudos." Also, seriously. "It's all good." It's all good? Really? Like, no matter what? Let go of the catchy catchphrases. Aah, isn't that better? Now, let's go make up our own.

Shine Your Shoes
Shining your old shoes
makes them look fantastic
and will make you feel
instantly spiffy

In a pinch, you can rub your leather shoes with the inside of a banana skin, then buff with a clean, soft cloth.

FINDING INSPIRATION:
YOUR FRIENDS AND
ACQUAINTANCES

WHO KNOWS WHERE I'D BE OH THOSE MANY YEARS AGO IF I hadn't seen that striking Korean woman at the noodle joint, who had her hair piled up in a loose upsweep, which was ingeniously clipped together with one of those big-hinged comb clips? Which caused me to immediately race to the drugstore to buy myself a big clippy comb? And that photograph I saw when I was in my teens, a beautiful black-and-white portrait of some Italian woman with the largest, most beautiful nose I had ever seen. Suddenly, my nose seemed elegant. Significant. It was a significant nose. In fact, compared to this fabulous, regal woman, my own, formerly enormous nose was suddenly not really big enough.

I think we all have those women in our lives who, at one time or another, influenced or nudged our perceptions about beauty and style. Sometimes it's just a glimpse of a photograph, or a moment in time, like that red-cheeked woman with the beautiful toothy smile and the knit cap on the bus with her daughter; or that lanky girl with the leather jacket and short ringlets, getting off her Vespa. She was the coolest thing on two wheels. Honestly, I wanted nothing more than to have long legs and short ringlets after I saw her. Once, at a stoplight in Echo Park, Los Angeles, a woman crossed the street in front of my car. She was short and not svelte, probably in her forties, with a tight sweater encasing a very round belly. She wore a tight pencil skirt and a pair of mules, on which she confidently sashayed. She owned that crosswalk. And I thought, that looks so good! Suddenly it occurred to me, wait a minute . . . this woman and I are of a very similar height and body type, her belly is way poochier than mine . . . and yet, I think I'm too fat to wear a tight skirt and sweater . . . heeey! A little lightbulb went off, and I bought myself a tight pencil skirt and started weaning myself off baggy dresses and oversize T-shirts.

Sometimes it's someone we know who ends up having an effect on our sense of style. Marjorie Magnani, who lived across the street from where I grew up in San Francisco, for instance. She had a collection of baby-doll heads, which completely enthralled me. She wore handwoven shawls and dangly earrings, and had a Noguchi coffee table. A real Noguchi table. Noguchi gave it to her. I didn't know that, of course, when I was ten years old. I just knew I liked to go to her house and look at her giant loom, and hang out in her kitchen.

Here's what I remember about Mara Simmons, who died when we were seventeen: I met Mara in kindergarten or first grade, I can't remember. Her best friend was Jennifer Cowan, who lived around the corner from me with her fabulous, ballet-dancing mom. Mara lived in the upstairs flat of a narrow building next door to the Vogue Theater in San Francisco. The Vogue

Theater ran *A Man and a Woman* for about a hundred years. Every time I think of the Vogue Theater, the theme from *A Man and a Woman* goes through my head (dah, dah, dah . . . na na na na na—na na na na na—dah, dah, dah . . . na na na na na—na na na na na, and so on) even though I never saw the movie. I'm sure it got into my head through osmosis, or genetics, or something.

Mara, Jennifer, and I used to play The Beatles. I mean, we really played The Beatles. Jennifer had a set of Beatle wigs, and we'd put on the Beatle wigs and argue over who got to be Paul and who got to be John, because Paul and John were supposedly the cutest and most popular. Sometimes I wanted to be George, because he was cute but kind of an underdog. None of us wanted to be Ringo. He was just too dorky, I guess. I was already a dork—I didn't want to have to play one in a wig, too. Mara didn't mind playing Ringo, because she didn't feel like a dork. She was extremely pretty, and discussed things as a grown-up would. Up to that point in my life, I had never heard a child say the word "nauseous," but was very impressed when Mara said it. I hoped I would have an opportunity to use it. Nauseous. I'm feeling nauseous. It sounded so sophisticated, at the age of six, to be feeling nauseous.

Mara's parents had given her *Rubber Soul,* The Beatles' new album, for her seventh birthday. There was a party, and the coffee table was moved out of the way so we could all dance the twist. I think Mitchell Yamamoto was there, in the same salt-and-pepper pants he wore *every day* to school. Kindergarten through sixth grade, rain or shine, Mitchell Yamamoto in the same white shirt, navy-blue cardigan, salt-and-pepper pants, and shiny, sensible black Oxford shoes. This was a public school, by the way. But Mitchell Yamamoto wore his own custom uniform. If it's true that the dorkiest among us end up being the most interesting and successful, then Mitchell Yamamoto must be the king of something.

Mara's mother was exotic and beautiful and wore turtleneck sweaters and slim pants and big hoop earrings and eyeliner, with her hair in a thick braid down her back. Mara's dad was called Specs and here is my favorite thing: on one wall of their San Francisco flat, which wasn't huge or anything, there was a built-in half-table, with a vase on top. And if you pushed gently on one side of this wall, it would open up, revealing a secret room that stretched the length of the apartment. I had always dreamed of having a secret room in my house, and here was a secret room, right in Mara's upstairs flat. The secret room was probably built in the 1920s, maybe to stash hooch during Prohibition, and it was long and narrow, just wide enough for Specs's reading chair and a lamp. We weren't allowed to play in there if Specs was inside. Years later, he opened a bar in North Beach, called Specs.

Then there's my friend Bella, who is an inspiration in ways too numerous to mention, but one thing is, she applies eyeliner beautifully. Not because she applies it perfectly. She's a wonderful artist, but she doesn't apply her eyeliner perfectly. I am able to apply eyeliner perfectly, but then I see Bella's eyeliner and it always looks better. Possibly because she's French, and has the most gorgeous nose, but also because her eyeliner looks as if it was applied while sitting on the deck of her barge after slipping on her sandals and grabbing her market bag. It's that artfully hurried-in-a-relaxed-way look, a beautiful afterthought, not at all a perfect line. An eyeliner that says, "I have got so many more important things to do, like finish my pastel drawing and cook some lovely fish. I'm French. Have another glass of wine." That is how eyeliner should be applied.

My friend Maria has quite possibly read everything ever written in this known universe, and has a vocabulary that could make a less literate person want to go crying home to Mama, or hole up with the OED for about a hundred years. But she would never let that happen. She would take that less literate person by the hand and assume that if they love books, they love books as much as she does, and she would engage that person in a long and really fun conversation about books. Maria adores David Foster Wallace and P. G. Wodehouse with equal fervor, and she is the only person I know (outside my dead British uncle) who can not only remember long passages and pithy quotes from various literary works, she will sprinkle in a quote from some play that was written in 1790 when she's having a regular conversation. But the quote is always appropriate, and she does it out of her sheer love of language, not out of some kind of highbrow notion of literary superiority. I, too, aspire to lobbing amusing, relevant three-hundred-year-old quotes into my conversations, but I can never seem to remember the quotes, which are probably stuck somewhere in my amygdala along with an assortment of jokes and their punch lines.

There's my pal Erika; when she talks, it's as if she has a huge, wonderful mouthful of interesting words she just can't wait to spill, and so I am always interested in what she has to say. She's an excellent writer, and speaks in a very writerly way without somehow sounding twee and pretentious.

All of my friends are wonderful, each in their own different ways, and I'm sure yours are, too. Although maybe you don't have a French friend who applies eyeliner well, and it's entirely possible that you wish I would just stop talking about all these people you don't know. Your mother does that all the time, and it's really annoying. But the thing is, we all need to grab our inspiration where we can find it. We are drawn to certain friends because we hope to catch a little bit of what they've got, just as we are drawn to sights, to smells, to images we see around us every day. Just as you surround yourself with people you love, surround yourself with things you love and that inspire you. Collect images from magazines, go to museums; fill yourself up with inspiration from friends, books, movies, travel, and people-watching. Use all this inspiration to add yet another interesting layer to yourself and your life.

MORE TIPS FROM THE FABULOUS OVER-FORTY SET

When I am having a dinner party, my husband often accuses me of "forgetting dessert." I may have pulled together a delicious gourmet feast, but apparently, for many people, the meal is not complete unless they can eat a plate of something sweet, gooey, and preferably chocolate. I would rather have the taste of garlic in my mouth for a while, or another glass of wine; I just don't have much of a sweet tooth, so I forget that other people do. A few friends of mine are deft at desserts, able to whisk together cakes and pies and puddings with as much enthusiasm as I caramelize onions and sauté mushrooms. If I'm inviting any of them for dinner, and if they offer to bring something, I will often ask them to bring one of those desserts they make so well, if it's not too much trouble. It's usually not too much trouble, and I'm always so grateful. And so is everyone else.

In that spirit, I thought I'd pose a handful of questions to a handful of interesting, over-the-age-of-forty women. Because, just as I "forget the dessert," I forget that other women like to wear shoes, or they might have their own thoughts about hair and lipstick, thoughts that might not mirror my own. A number of them just may have some really good tricks that I might not know. I find that hard to believe, but it's possible. Some of them live in a colder climate than I, so they're good with things like "boots" and "coats" since there's not much call for that sort of thing where I live. Maybe you'll get a few good ideas from them, in case you have found my years of extensive research into red lipstick completely useless to you.

I asked them about their default outfit, and what they still like to wear even if they might secretly think they "shouldn't." I asked them to reveal their "Best Secret Beauty Tips," tips they might've wished they'd known when they were twenty, but they know now. I asked my sister Jane about her secret beauty tips; Jane is over fifty but looks much younger. Like, way younger. Weirdly way younger. I think it's because she has kept her body so busy it kind of lost track of birthdays and it still thinks it's about thirty-two. She claims it's the "loads of fresh mountain air, exercise, and washing my face using only clean water, no soap, and a scrub when necessary. Cream and sunscreen. Keep it simple." She makes no mention of a portrait in the attic, or a secret serum from outer space. So I guess a little mountain air is in order.

Most of the "secret beauty tips" were variations on the "keep it simple" theme, but all of the advice should provide at least a spoonful of inspiration, a new bit of information to add to your store, or even a little reinforcement for what you're already doing.

What's your best secret beauty trick?

When your skin is blah, you can do a really fast facial by smoothing cold cream or olive oil on your face and, with a small heap of sugar, on your left palm, give yourself a great exfoliation. Cornmeal works too, but sugar melts down the drain quickly.

—LESLIE

My best advice, I guess, is to take it easy on the eye makeup . . . maybe don't wear it every day. Taking it off is very hard on that delicate skin, I think. My friends who use a lot of eye makeup every day have tugged their eyelids all to hell.

—MARIA

I like to look carefree and naturally gracious. I only wear clothes I'm comfortable in. I stay away from clothes being too tight, or wearing shoes that hurt. I like to accentuate the shape of my eyes with liquid eyeliner. A touch of red and/or pink in my clothing or accessories is always a plus.

—BELLA

1. Brow powder and red lipstick. Keep makeup simple. Load it on, and you look like an old pastry.

2. Stand up straight.

3. Smile more. In my early twenties, I was living in Paris with my much older boyfriend, who took me to Agnès B to buy me a birthday present. I tried on this long black cotton dress with long, long sleeves. It looked like the kind of thing a character might have worn to a festive barn raising in Witness. *I turned to the attractive forty- or fiftysomething saleslady and said, "Um . . . well . . . it's so . . . black," and she said, "Well, mademoiselle, you'll just have to smile more." It was then that I knew this was the post-thirty-five woman's secret ammo.*

—ALEXANDRA

Sleep, sleep, sleep!

—SUSANNA

Use an eyelash curler. It wakes up your eyes even if you've had a shitty night's sleep. (And don't bother with the cheap ones. They don't work.)

—WENDY

I mix foundation with moisturizer in the palm of my hand.

—JOYCE

*Be healthy and dive into those pockets of happiness that come
your way. When you feel good, you look good. Cliché, but
true.*

—DIANA

Mineral powder sunscreen, for the face.
—RUTH

*Never leave the house looking like shit, which means put on
some lipstick that suits you, and sunglasses.*

—JANET

*Raw-honey facials! Just smear some on, sit for fifteen
minutes, then rinse off with warm water. Like a $120 facial!*
—ERIKA

And my friend Garen Tolkin, who is a makeup artist, has an
unusual beauty trick to help you look like Madame X, which I
am going to try immediately:

*I love rosy cheeks. I want to look like I stepped out of a
Gainsborough. I long to look like a painting by John Singer
Sargent. And all their women have rosy—even blotchy cheeks.
So why does it look so beautiful on them and so horrible on
me? The real problem is our red blotchy necks. All the great
painted beauties have white necks! So my trick is this: only
use foundation on your neck, and don't forget to extend
beyond your ears onto the back of your neck. Blend it up to
your jawline. Smooth and smooth (adding a dab, perhaps,*

on the sides of your chin and behind your nose wings). Keep
it subtle. Use your clean, slightly-moistened-with-cool-water
hands to smooth and blend. Don't forget your chest. This
is best done when you are just out of the shower, or at least
naked. Then lightly blot excess with a tissue. Lightly. Then,
using a great big powder puff dipped into the finest loose
translucent powder (shaking off the excess)—finish it into a
glowing, kissable surface. You'll be amazed. Add a little blush
to your cheeks, curl your eyelashes, rouge your lips, and you
too can have the skin of a Renoir!

What is your uniform? Do you have a uniform? That easy outfit you know you can pull together in a matter of minutes that makes you feel pulled together?

I asked this question about the uniform because I have always
liked the concept of having my own self-styled uniform. When
I was younger, I loved the idea of wearing a white Oxford shirt,
black slacks, and a suit jacket, preferably in black or dark blue
cashmere. But the reality of me in a mannish suit was quite different from the picture in my head; apparently, it helps to be
long, lanky, and wafer-thin. When you are under 5'2" and have
visible hips, wearing an Oxford shirt and a suit is not necessarily
the most flattering, nor is it the most, er, feminine look. I have
sadly given up my dream of wearing a suit like Marlene Dietrich
(how did she do it? Oh. That's right.), but it did get me thinking
about the whole idea of "uniforms" for women, since women
(unless you wear a real uniform for work) don't have the closet
full of suits that most men have.

Do I have a uniform? My own default throw-it-on outfit that comes to mind is a skirt and a sweater: my black cashmere cardigan, buttoned up but open at the neck and worn as a shirt, with a dark brown jersey skirt or a black mid-calf pencil skirt, or a pair of capris. Hair pulled back in a twist, red lipstick and powder, and my black peacoat if it's cold. Something flat and comfortable on my feet. Here's what a few friends have to say:

I wear a column of something nearly monochromatic plus a great jacket. Pants pants pants. If I am feeling even slightly iffy, I wear pants. And one piece of jewelry, but noteworthy.

—LESLIE

Whatever my favorite black pants of the moment with a beautiful shirt or sweater. Good earrings. Bright lipstick. Eyeliner!

—ERIKA

Little black dress (I have literally dozens: wool, silk, cotton; sleeveless, mostly). Black hose (or no hose), black stiletto heels, and a cardigan, or a coat, or my pashmina.

—MARIA

Pencil/A-line skirt, cashmere sweater/peasant blouse, stilettos/knee-length boots, chignon.

—ALEXANDRA

Jeans, black cashmere sweater, and sandals or boots, depending on the season.

—Susanna

Anything black, with silver jewelry.

—Ruth

Fitted slim pants with a bold pattern, no pockets, a solid fitted T-shirt, flats, and a rockin' necklace. A smallish cardigan. Hair in a ponytail is awful but still haven't come up with a proper, hip "do" for my age.

—Gail

Black, black, black and jeans with black.

—Marla

My uniform by day includes nice panties (this comes from my mother, who said it was important to always have nice clean underwear on—she had gorgeous Pucci panties and bras), a bra that works, a favorite soft T-shirt, jeans, and boots, or my orange Converse sneakers. By night, nice underwear again (of course), a little brown dress I have that hits me at the knee, purple tights, and leg-hugging brown suede boots with a slight heel. I loathe most or all accessories— belts, scarves, bangles—though I always wear a ring on my right hand.

—Diana

*Boots from October to April. A new pair each year; I have
six or seven. Sometimes short, sometimes tall. Jeans that fit
really well, and shirts that are beautiful. Summer, skirts and
T-shirts.*

—JOYCE

*Black will often do the trick when I don't have the time to
put an outfit together. I know I can add a red necklace or a
colorful headband in my black hair and ho la la.*

—BELLA

*Buffalo jeans with a comfy gray cashmere pullover. Dress
it up with heels and jewelry or just wear flip-flops. Always
works for me.*

—JANE

*NO! I hate uniforms. I'm too much like Sybil and clothes help
in my transformation.*

—SHANTÉ

What do you instinctively know you "shouldn't" wear, now that you've reached a certain age?

Alexandra, Gail, Jane, Susanna, Ruth, Marla, Janet, Bella, Joyce,
Wendy, Maria, Geri, Shanté (and I) all weigh in:

Miniskirts
Huge hoop earrings
Leg o' mutton sleeves
Lamé

Skirts above the middle of my knees. Sleeveless
anything.

Clothes my children wear, clothes found in the section
where all the young skinny girls are

I know that I can't wear short shorts, minis, bikinis,
or—for the most part—things without sleeves

I love 1960s style A-line miniskirts in bright prints, but
now I have "puppy dog face" knees (kneecap is the
nose, the saggy part above for the eyes) but I still try
them on when I see one that I love, and enjoy the
look in the privacy of the dressing room

Baby-doll dresses

Bare midriff

High-waisted mom jeans

Above-the-knee Bermuda shorts

Puffy-sleeved anything

RUFFLES

A very short nightie, and very high heels, because I feel
stupid if I can't walk in them, and if I feel stupid, I
look silly

Oversize clothing. Used to look really cute in my
twenties. Now? Oh dear.

And, of course, my friend Shanté (who's feisty) took umbrage
at the whole idea that she "shouldn't" be wearing something,
and replied with this: "Instinctively, I should wear everything
I want exactly because I HAVE REACHED THAT CERTAIN
AGE!! And bikinis!! Because damn it, I look good in them!"

What do you still wear—even though you know you "shouldn't"—because it makes you happy?

Converse low-tops, skinny jeans, pigtails, my favorite 1968 Empire-waist aquamarine muumuu.

—ALEXANDRA

I still wear my orangey-red "Smith's Jeans" T-shirt from Lucky Brand jeans because I love the color.

—WENDY

I wear slinky, strappy camisoles with a partly buttoned shirt on top. I think, shoot, if they want to stare at my nipples, that's their problem. I would never have done that at twenty-five.

—LESLIE

I don't wear miniskirts anymore, though some of my mates do . . . but I'll never give up my sky-high heels.

—MARIA

All my peasant blouses!
—SUSANNA

Short dresses and skirts, not supershort, but a little above the knees—with textured patterned tights.

—RUTH

Tight stretch jeans, boot cut, slightly off the hip. Why? My friends and husband say I look good in them (and I trust that they are not just being nice) and mostly because at fifty-seven, you need something casual to wear in the evening that's slightly hip. Why maybe I shouldn't? When jeans fit in the hips perfectly, those love handles get pushed up above the waistband, and if you are wearing a nice, slightly fitted T-shirt top, you get that spare-tire bulge thing happening. When I want to lose a few pounds, it's not the scale or size I'm looking at, it's what's above that waistband.

—GAIL

I still wear lingerie and thongs because although I don't look as good as I used to, I don't look bad for someone my age, and it makes me feel oh so sexy.

—JANE

I know I shouldn't walk around without a bra but I happily do, never regretting it unless someone unexpectedly pops over.

—GERI

Even though I am thin and 5'9", it doesn't mean I should wear a miniskirt with high heels. Short skirts with flats, longer skirts with high heels. Please.

—JOYCE

My hair in two braids.

—CHRISTIE

I wear no clothes. (I really shouldn't!)
—MARLA

HERE'S A BEAUTY TIP FROM ME

Wash your face every night before bed. That's right, it's hard to believe, but a lot of women are going to bed without washing their faces. I know! It just makes me crazy. But okay, you know who you are, and I want to help. Clean your face before your head hits that pillow. And if you make a point of cleaning your face a few hours before your head hits that pillow, it's more apt to get done. If it's really late and you've been to a party and all you want to do is to climb into bed with all your clothes on and drift off into dreamland, still: dampen a few balls of cotton with a little water and some almond oil (which of course you always keep by your bathroom sink for such an occasion) and wipe the grime from your face and neck. Gently rub in a circular motion until there is nothing visible left on the cotton balls. At this point, it's safe to get into bed, and the remnants of the almond oil will keep your face moisturized until you can do a bang-up job in the morning. Then again, as long as you're in there, you could cover your face with a warm washcloth, because that would feel really good, wouldn't it? And if you put on some nice eye cream at this point, and dab on a few dabs of night cream, I mean, you're up, right? You might as well, and your skin will be so much happier and feel so much more nourished in the morning. Cleansing your face before bed will keep your pores clean and lovely, and your skin will just last longer, really. Wash it gently with a little Cetaphil or some cleansing oil. Use a scrub if you're feeling especially ambitious. Rinse. Spray on some mineral water or Na-PCA, so your face is a little moist when you put on your super-duper moisturizing night cream. And in the morning, you won't need to bring in the heavy artillery.

A CHEAP AND AMUSING BEAUTY TIP

We all know we're not supposed to pick at our blackheads and squeeze our pimples and peel our sunburns, but apparently there's something very satisfying to a lot of women about the picking and peeling. My friend Garen Tolkin is a professional makeup artist, so she knows a lot about making people look beautiful; she tells me she's always telling women not to "pick" at things on their faces. I am not a picker, but perhaps some of you are pickers. Well, my friend Garen has got the best alternative, which will satisfy your need to pick and peel, while simultaneously being good for your skin. Go out and buy some Freeman Cucumber Facial Peel-Off Mask, available at the drugstore. Dab it on problem spots on your face whenever you are feeling in a particularly picky mood. Let it dry, then pick and peel to your heart's content. Garen says, "It's the cheapest possible beauty aid, but the only one that works as well or provides as gratifying an activity!"

NEW YEAR'S RESOLUTIONS

I THINK NEW YEAR'S DAY IS A PERFECT TIME TO SIT DOWN with your thoughts and a pad of paper, and make a list of everything you'd like to accomplish in the upcoming year. But sometimes New Year's Day turns out to be exactly not the right time to sit down and do anything. In fact, you would prefer to lie down, with a very soft pillow and a cool compress over your eyes, and get some much-needed extra sleep. Or perhaps you're wide-awake and ready to face the day, but you find you've got relatives in your guest room and on your sofa, and one sleeping on the floor of the rumpus room. You don't really have a rumpus room, but at some point on New Year's Eve, everyone thought it would be a good idea to upend the living room and play that game you used to play when you were kids, where you put cushions all over the place and everyone has to get around without touching the floor. You will also have to dismantle the "fort" someone made out of blankets and chairs, sooner or later—and it just doesn't look as if there's going to be enough time today to light a candle, sip some mint tea, and jot down your fondest hopes for the New Year.

But don't despair; just as you're allowed to say "Happy New Year!" for the entire month of January, you have the entire month of January to come up with some resolutions. The Buddhist New Year falls on the first full moon in January, so you can cut yourself a little slack if you've procrastinated. Chinese New Year usually falls sometime between the latter part of January and the early part of February, and is another fine occasion to make some resolutions, in case you never got around to it on the first of the month. Plus, Chinese New Year comes with a lot of nice decorations, delicious food, and some really good superstitions and rituals. Tibetan New Year is in late February and lasts for three days, giving you not only one more reason to celebrate but also you've bought yourself quite a bit of extra time for those resolutions. The Rosicrucian New Year is celebrated on the Spring Equinox, which is a lovely time to celebrate new beginnings, even if you aren't a strict pagan. And if you really just blew off the whole thing, you still have the Jewish New Year, which falls sometime toward the end of September or the beginning of October.

And why do we need to make resolutions? Well, we don't *have* to. But I'm a big believer in lists, and New Year's resolutions are the ultimate list. Instead of

Call the plumber
Groceries
Bills
Pick up toilet paper

we can get down all of our personal intentions, goals that may be slightly deeper and more personal than "replace toothbrush" or "loaf of bread, peanut butter, bananas." And sometimes just putting your intentions down on paper helps nudge them along.

SPEAKING OF LISTS: *UNE FÊTE DE REVE*

My friend Gail, who taught me this, calls it a JAKA. When I tried it a few times with my friend Maria, we called it Mission: Control. When I did it with my friend Thompy, we called it "that four-quadrant-list thingy." Whatever you call it, it's a fun and practical exercise to do with one of your good friends. So here's how it's done:

You meet once a month with a friend who has agreed to be your partner in this venture. Each person gets twenty uninterrupted minutes to talk about the things that are troubling them and areas where they need work. Just to talk through it. Then you set goals in four areas: personal, family, financial, and career/work. Write your goals in four quadrants on a piece of paper, or an index card, or a little business card. Put it where you'll be able to see it every day. Then set the date for your next meeting. When you meet next, you have the twenty minutes to each report on what you've accomplished and how you are doing. Then you set new goals in your four quadrants.

Meet your good friend over a pot of tea or a tasty meal. Meet in the morning for coffee, or meet in the late afternoon for a glass of wine. The point is, meet somewhere pleasant and comfortable, either your house or your friend's house, or a coffeehouse, or a café by a park. You'll sit across from your friend, and you'll each get twenty minutes to speak, uninterrupted. The idea is that you will write down your intentions, which gives them heft and reality—and you'll have a real, live witness as you state your intentions aloud. (While simultaneously sipping some really nice hot chocolate, say, and nibbling on a madeleine.)

Write down only one or two things you would like to accomplish each month; three at the most. For instance, under "family," you might say something like, "bring the boys to the library once a week," or "Sunday music nights," or "call Mom and Dad every Friday." Under "personal," you'll put down anything having to do with you, personally, something that is meant to feed you alone. "Get a massage." "Walk for twenty minutes every day." "Listen to meditation tape." "Take hula lessons." "Get new running shoes." "Research French classes." "Daily nap." "Dance in underwear." You get the idea. Under "financial," you'll put down one or two pressing financial goals. "Save $100 a month for vacation." "Talk to bank about refinancing." "Research higher interest-earning account." Under "career" or "work," you will put down anything pertaining to your career, whether it's "set up Web site," "do promotional mailer," "revise résumé," "organize and clean studio," or whatever it is that's relevant to your particular career. But, of course, you won't list everything, just one or two things.

If you put down a whole long list, you will be overwhelmed. Because, honestly, are you really going to take hula lessons, learn French, exercise every day, get a weekly massage, and lose ten pounds in one month? No, you are not. You will be only setting yourself up for frustration and self-loathing. So write down just one or two things that you really want to accomplish, even if you think they're very small goals. Walking for fifteen minutes every day may seem like some kind of sissy goal compared to "run a 10K" or "train for a triathlon," but if you have generally got your behind glued to a computer chair—only rising occasionally to fetch a tumbler of water or snatch a handful of granola—then fifteen minutes a day of walking is a lofty goal. Think specifically rather than generally. This is how my friend Gail explains it. She's been doing it for about ten years with her friend Suzette:

> The name is JAKA, from a book that I read years ago, called Just A K.I.S.S. Away, A Woman's Guide to Winning the Money Game by Linda Cline Chandler. We usually have a meal and wine at Suzette's house or mine, but at the beginning of the year we go out and have a really nice dinner to start fresh and to treat ourselves. The thing that we do on the first JAKA meeting of the year is to present and read a journal page that we've written the previous year: For instance, last year—as close to January 1st as possible—we envisioned it being the last day of the current year, as if the new year was just ending. We wrote in the present tense about all the wonderful things that "happened" from the four quadrants. So this year I read what I wrote last year: "It is New Year's Eve, and I'm so glad that Cynthia is healthy again (she is) and that Piet and I completed our wonderful addition. I love my new office and he loves his (didn't happen). Thank God I got those two new Sugar Cove Jobs (I did) as I love working on the North Shore. I was able to

*save. . . . My time with Mom was wonderful . . ." and so on,
like that. You see if whatever you envisioned came to fruition
for you. It's so much fun. I wrote one for this year that I
will put away and read at our January JAKA next year. We
made this all up based on the book and added fun things, like
occasionally we will take a little JAKA trip somewhere as a
reward. It has helped in every area of our lives. Especially
with things that seemed impossible to accomplish or the
things we were fearful of doing.*

So Gail's JAKA is really like doing monthly New Year's resolutions. Or glorified to-do lists. I know it sounds kind of ooga-booga,
but she swears by the practice, and says that it's eerie how well it
works. And my friend Gail is the salt of the earth, so I believe her.

If you decide to try this with a friend, customize it to your
own taste. Give it your own name. (When I start up again, I'm
going to call it *Fête de Reves*, which, loosely translated, means "a
feast of dreams," which sounds very poetic in French, as do so
many things. Unless you're a French person, in which case it may
sound more romantic in Latvian or Italian.) Make your own ritual around it. See if it works for you. If nothing else, it's a lovely
chance to sit with a friend and pick at a few nagging problems.

GIVE YOURSELF A PERMISSION SLIP

I hereby grant you permission to wear whatever you
    want to wear to bed, then wake up and wear the
    same thing all day long

I hereby grant you permission to eat chocolate

I hereby grant you permission to not do the elliptical
machine today

I hereby grant you permission to not take your work
home tonight

I hereby grant you permission to meet your friends for
lunch and have a glass of wine, even if it's noon

I hereby grant you permission to play hooky and see a
movie this morning

I hereby grant you permission for you to just say no, for
a change

I hereby grant you permission to skip your flossing
tonight

I hereby grant you permission to go to sleep at seven
thirty P.M.

I hereby grant you permission to read in bed all
morning

I hereby grant you permission to ask for help

PART II

I'VE BEEN TO A MARVELOUS PARTY

HERE'S HOW YOU DO IT: BIRTHDAYS

OKAY, WE GET—WHAT? IF WE'RE LUCKY, SIXTY OR SEVENTY birthdays? Maybe eighty or ninety, if we're very, very fortunate? That is not very many birthdays, in the big scheme of things. Even if you lived to be a hundred and ten, that is still only one hundred and ten opportunities to celebrate. If you were to celebrate all of those birthdays in one year, there wouldn't be much more than three months' worth of celebration. And then it would be over! Three months! Out of your WHOLE LIFE. What I'm getting at here is, why don't you like to celebrate your birthday? Here you get one day per year—*one day*—where you get to be the Queen of the World. At least Queen of Your Little World. For heaven's sake, let people know!

Friends will give you little gifts, and will want to take you out to breakfast and lunch. They will sing to you on your phone answering machine. Parties can be held, even on weeknights. Boyfriends, husbands, or partners will see to your dining needs, and you will probably get to eat exactly where and what you want to eat. Unless they surprise you, which is also absolutely great, as it is just one more way you know that they are thinking of you. People might bring you flowers, or perfume, or a hand-made picture. People will want to do things for you! I swear, they will encourage you to get a massage or a pedicure. They will pour champagne, and toast to your health! They really want you to have *Your Special Day*. What could possibly be bad about that? Is there a downside I'm just not seeing?

Yes, it's true, you are now a year older. Perhaps you'd rather not draw attention to that. But the fact is, you will be one year older, party or no party. So why not have a party? Oh, you don't really like parties. You just don't want to "make a big deal" out of your birthday. You have socks to fold. You don't want to *put people out*. Okay, fine. You don't have to have a party, although I think you're just being ornery. But at least take the day off—it's your birthday!

If your birthday falls on a weekday and you really can't take the day off because you might get in trouble at work or something, then you have special dispensation to have your birthday be the beginning of your Birthday Week. In fact, since we get so few days to celebrate in our lifetimes, I suggest we should all get to have a Birthday Week. If your birthday should fortuitously fall on a Friday or Saturday night, you can decide whether you want to have a simple "Birthday Weekend," or if you'd rather take the entire week following your birthday as your Birthday Week. You may also use a Saturday birthday as the culmination of your Birthday Week, with many small celebrations leading up to the final birthday festivity. Either way, the Birthday Week alleviates the pressure of having to express all that pent-up celebratory feeling in one single birth *day*. If you're about to experience a birthday that involves a large zero, then why not make it a Birthday Month? Do something a little special for yourself every day of that month. Give yourself a daily permission slip to sit down and enjoy lunch with a friend, to go to the movies on a weeknight, to paint your toenails a color not found in nature, or to have a series of small gatherings with friends, so they can coo over you.

MARTY'S BOAT

I'm going to give you some really good ideas of things to do, because clearly you aren't going to think of what to do until the last minute, because you don't want to "make a fuss." But I'm telling you, make a fuss! If you won't do it for yourself, do it for your friends, because everyone likes to celebrate. Everyone is secretly looking for reasons to celebrate, a reason to put on a party dress, a reason to leave work behind, to eat and drink and laugh. And if you have friends you're afraid will roll their eyes at the idea of going to yet another birthday party, then they won't come! They will make a flimsy excuse, and they won't be there, which will be great! Because then you won't have to run around worrying about whether or not they're having a good time, and there will be more cake for you.

Perhaps you told everyone you really don't want to make a big deal of your birthday, but you're secretly hoping and actually expecting your loved ones to plan and carry out a fabulous and elaborate surprise party. Then your birthday arrives. You wake up with a sort of wistful anticipation in your heart, and go about your day coyly, expectantly, with a little flutter in your tummy.

By ten o'clock that night, you are finishing up a bottle of cheap Prosecco left over from New Year's Eve, and wiping off a messy tears 'n' snot combo with the soggy sleeve of your bathrobe. You eventually fall asleep on the sofa, angry at the world and hating all your friends. So you can see why it's a good idea to sort of plan ahead. As a wise friend once said (thanks, Raz!), "Know what you want or you'll get what you get."

In fact, it's a good idea to think up about a million things that you'd like to do to celebrate your birthday. Then narrow it down to maybe twenty. And then sit with your list and think about each thing on your list, and how you would feel doing it, and how you can make it happen. And then you might narrow your list down some more, or add to it. The point is, you're taking this opportunity—your birthday—to celebrate yourself! So think of how you might best celebrate yourself, and then figure out if it's something you want to do on your actual birthday, or over the course of the week leading up to, or following, your birthday.

When my youngest son turned eight, he made a list of what he wanted to do on his birthday. This was his list:

Wake up and have a Surprise Breakfast
Kayaking with Thompy and Marty (I get to be in
    Marty's boat)
Sushi for dinner
A back rub
Watch a movie
Stay up late

The boy really knows how to take care of himself. If you haven't been taking care of yourself in a similar fashion since you were eight years old, perhaps it's time to start. Now, all of us can't be lucky enough to "be in Marty's boat." To "be in Marty's boat" means you get to sit in the front of my friend Martin's kayak and paddle while experiencing a barrage of colorful pirate badinage, such as: "ROW! ROW, YOU SCURVY KNAVE!" and "FASTER, YOU STINKIN' LANDLUBBER!" For about two solid hours. Honestly, it never gets old. Sadly, all of you don't get to do this, only a fortunate few. But surely you have your own version of Marty's boat.

I am going to have a very big birthday next month. A birthday involving a zero. My birthday will fall on a Monday, which gives me a little challenge: do I have a party on the Saturday *before* my birthday? Do I have a party on the Saturday *after* my birthday? Do I have several small gatherings? Do I have a party at all? So, to give you an example, let's just pretend my birthday is Monday, March 9. My list might look something like this:

I. Sunday, March 8, Birthday Eve

    A. Go to the marina with R and the boys and watch the boats in the channel. Walk down the beach. Dinner at Hot Dog on a Stick.

II. Monday, March 9, Birthday!!!

    A. Get pounces and kisses from R and boys. Go back to sleep. Sleep in, but not too late. Ride bike to Bloom, meet Wendy for breakfast. Ride bike to beach? Walk with Thompy if she's in town? Museum?

B. Olympic spa for scrubbing and pounding by burly Korean woman.

C. Come home. Put feet up. When boys come home, command cello performance of youngest son who promised me a good song for my birthday. Command oldest son to accompany me on The Kinks' song "Village Green." Group hug. More songs! Tea.

D. Head to the Farmer's Market and meet small group of friends whom I have alerted to come celebrate. Buy bottle of Malbec. Make Peter sing *"Feliz Anniversario"* in Portuguese. Bask in birthday wishes. Ask R to play a song. Stay until market closes. Have Thompy for a sleepover.

E. Head home. Make fire in fireplace. Make R play one more song. Stay up late with Thompy and discuss trip to Paris, epiphanies, new projects, and what happens next.

III. Tuesday through Friday, March 10–13
  A. Paint a birthday self-portrait

  B. Continue to plot out previously mentioned trip to Paris that I am hoping to give myself for my birthday (in which I will fly to Paris, rent a small boat, and live on it for three weeks with the boys).

  C. Find friend to ride bikes to the beach. Make martinis for friends. Sing with Doug, John, Peter, and Henry.

Meet Bella at the market. Morning movies with Lisa and Wendy. Do a drawing with Atticus. Read a good book.

IV. **Saturday, March 14**

   A. Maybe a little cocktail party, to end fabulous Birthday Week. Cocktails and food and music. Get boys to pass hors d'oeuvres. Everyone has to bring guitars, ukes, accordions, drums. Twinkle lights in the trees! See how much it would cost to have someone clean up afterward. Bartender? So I don't have to spend all night mixing cocktails. Borrow a slide carousel, and have a loop of old slides showing on a wall. Dance with everyone. Suck helium out of balloons and talk funny. Sing songs with helium voices.

Some of what I have on my list is wishful thinking, and some of it depends on what my financial situation is around the time of my birthday. If it turns out I can't afford the works at a local spa, then I'll get a $40 massage at the Thai place, and then come home and take a hot bath. If the cheap massage is out of the question, I'll ask my son to rub my shoulders. If it turns out that I'm unable to spring for a fully catered and bartended birthday party bash, I can still invite my friends over. Friends are usually happy to bring a bottle of wine, and if you ask a few friends to bring something to eat in lieu of a birthday gift, no one will go hungry. If you have musical friends, ask them to bring their instruments. If not, come up with your own dance party mix, or have some Bach playing quietly in the background.

If you really don't want your friends to give you gifts but you know they will insist on it, ask for something else instead. Like their time: a lunch with one, a night at the movies with another.

Now, what would I do if money were no object and I had no work deadlines and I didn't have to help get my kids off to school and do grocery shopping and feed a family? I'd rent a house right on the beach for a week, not too far from home—and have friends drop by at different times for a series of small gatherings and musical jam sessions. I'd have a little vacation there, and I'd take the time to plot my course for the upcoming year. I'd have it be at a beach that was near a store and some restaurants, so that I wouldn't have to get in the car if I didn't want to. I'd bring my bicycle and I'd go for a bike ride every day. I'd bring a sketch pad and plot out some paintings, and I'd write down some new ideas for books. I'd rent a kayak and go kayaking in the ocean. Maybe I'll save that for my next big birthday.

You can start planning now for *your* next birthday, mostly because it's really fun to do. You might end up finding out things about yourself you never knew. Who knew you always wanted to ride in a hot-air balloon? Had you ever before thought about how much fun it would be to spend the day riding roller-coasters? Or perhaps spending the day in quiet contemplation is your idea of heaven. Maybe meeting friends for a meal, or taking an entire day off to read a book. Planning your day might end up being half the fun.

And if any especially big birthdays were not celebrated in the way you had always hoped they would be, guess what? You get a do-over! You really do. I'm granting you a do-over. If you let a big one go by without telling anyone, and you realized too late that it was a really pathetic and sad way to spend a birthday; or if your busy and selfish "friends" neglected to throw you a surprise birthday ball, well, look at your calendar and plan yourself a little belated birthday weekend. It'll be like Christmas in July! Because it's never too late.

DINNER AT TIFFANY'S:
A BOOK GROUP IDEA TO MAKE
YOU EVEN MORE OF A NERD

WHENEVER IT'S MY TURN TO HOST A BOOK GROUP EVENING, I enjoy making a book-inspired thematic dinner. I know, it makes me sound like the kind of person I wouldn't want to be friends with, but it's so much fun, and it makes me happy, and everyone gets to eat well. Things got a little out of hand when we read Dostoyevsky and I felt impelled to make something called *"selyodka pod shouboy"* and some complicated dishes involving aspic. For dessert that evening, I made a Russian pineapple cake "served with a topping of greed, lust, squalor, and unredeemed suffering," along with vodka "infused with realism and intrigue," and a "Stinking Lizaveta cheese plate." It was a feast fit for a tsar, and twelve rowdy women who like Russian literature. Okay, so I went a little overboard. And not everyone loves pickled herring, I know, I know. They just don't. But a few people do, and those who do love it really, really loved it.

For each book-inspired dinner I make, I write up a menu. Which is what I did when we read Truman Capote's *Breakfast at Tiffany's*, a book I hadn't read for a long time. Not to be confused with the movie of the same name, which ends on a disconcertingly happy note.

If you yourself are not exactly Holly Golightly, if you have never been a Holly Golightly, you still might have had one in your life at some point. My friend Beth was my Holly Golightly. We spent one summer almost entirely together, and at the time, I had no idea why she found my company preferable to any of the far more fascinating people from the far more fascinating circles in which she circulated. People who apparently were "wild!" and "divine"; people who freely used adjectives like "wild!" and "divine" without at all feeling self-conscious.

My Holly was stunning, from Boston, with very short, white-bleached hair; alternately captivating and exasperating, either mysteriously impenetrable or maddeningly frivolous. But she had a gift to which I could only hope to aspire: she was a spellbinding raconteur, with the ability to make a hair-raising adventure story from the simplest errand.

Let's say we would spend an afternoon doing those banal but necessary things a girl must do when she is twenty-three and living in a warehouse downtown; the chores that must be undertaken if she wants to have a quick afternoon nap in order to be refreshed for the evening's festivities; festivities that usually involved finding a dance club around one A.M., dancing into the wee hours, searching for a dining establishment at four A.M., driving through the dry riverbed at five, and diving into the sofa, or a bed, somewhere in the vicinity of six A.M. Unless we found a cheap breakfast place first. We were busy girls. We'd wake up late and find some dive-y taco stand to take the edge off; maybe shop for adorably packaged food at that tiny Japanese market in

Little Tokyo: pickled ginger, mystery seaweed rolls, something pink and puffy from the refrigerated section. The basics. Then we'd do errands: a trip to the post office, for instance, to mail letters. (Remember letters? "Letters" are what we used to write before e-mail, and the post office is the place where a person could buy a "stamp" and "mail" a "letter." But you'll remember this, if you're close to my age.)

Anyway, later that night we'd be off to a club, or to a party, and at some point I would spot Beth regaling a group of captivated listeners with a story. An exciting story of a wild afternoon she spent downtown, when she was apparently almost hit by a car! And then this poetry-spouting homeless man waylaid her and proposed marriage! And then this adorable Latin boy at some taco stand gave her all this free food! And I would stand on the edge of the group listening, and I would suddenly realize that she was describing our trip to the post office: our uneventful little errand, where we stood in line and I got some stamps. I vaguely remembered Beth dodging a car, and there might have been an unfortunate homeless man with a shopping cart, and we might have had tacos for lunch. But, really, we just went to the post office. How had it turned into such a scintillating adventure? How could it be that everyone who heard Beth's story envied our trip to the post office and wished that their trips to the post office could be so fun-filled, so fraught with excitement and danger?

Any innocent walk to the corner newsstand would take on mythic proportions in Beth's hands, and our plucky, madcap exploits became the talk of the late-night cafés. I would stop by my little coffeehouse and, with a knowing wink, some near-

stranger would launch into an account he'd heard of some esca-
pade that Beth and I had undertaken. Perhaps it was the time we
went out for a carton of milk, or organized the canned goods.
Whatever we had done, it was fascinating. I, by extension, was
fascinating.

When I recently reread *Breakfast at Tiffany's,* I was reminded
of Beth, and the gift certain people have of presenting themselves to the world in the way they would like to be seen. Holly
Golightly was a master of it. It was agreed that she was a phony,
but that she was a "real" phony. The good kind: A genuine
phony. Who knows where she came from, but just like her cre-
ator, Truman Capote, she reinvented herself as a chic New York
party girl.

We can't all be Holly Golightly, because, frankly, darling, it's
hard work and entails too many late nights, too many lunches
of cottage cheese and melba toast, too many broken hearts, and
asking fat men for powder-room money and cab fare. But we
can be Holly Golightly once in a while, and we can invite some
divine friends over for a wild evening of cocktails and dinner,
and maybe the menu might look something like the one I've
come up with, or one you could come up with yourself.

It's really all about the presentation, darling—it's about
naming a dish. If you make a ham sandwich and call it a *croque
monsieur,* well, it sounds like a lot more fun, doesn't it? Miss
Golightly, in her momentary passion for the culinary arts,
tended toward the more outré: dishes requiring terrapin, pheasant, and saffron rice with chocolate sauce ("an East Indian classic, my dear"). Well, terrapin is endangered, last I heard; and
although I thought it might be fun to re-create the "tobacco

tapioca" described in the book, I don't think you need to sicken yourselves to properly capture the spirit of Holly Golightly. The dishes should be comforting; fancy-sounding on the outside but easy to make; yummy and possibly gooey on the inside. Things you can cook ahead of time, so you have more time to drink and visit with your fabulous, wild, divine friends.

Bon appétit!

DINNER AT TIFFANY'S MENU

COCKTAILS AND FINGER FOOD

"Mean Reds"
A spicy Manhattan cocktail made with Maker's Mark and a dash of hot pepper.

Martini Cocktail
Joe Bell's White Angel
Mixed Olive Tray
Drunken Goat Cheese with Melba Toast

ENTRÉE

Cold Chutney Meatloaf

Sally Tomatoes
Roasted organic cherry tomatoes with basil

Potatoes Golightly
Yukon Gold potatoes and turnips roasted with olive oil
and coarse salt

Lulamae's Briar Patch Salad
Oranges, red onions, and Moroccan olives tossed
with arugula and splashed with red wine vinegar and
walnut oil

Served with New York Merlot
Jamesport Vineyards

ABANDONING CATS IN THE RAIN

Rusty Trawler's Raw Baby Buttocks
Pear pudding made with vanilla and yogurt

Coffee or Tea
100-year-old brandy
(if not available, more wine)

DINNER AT TIFFANY'S RECIPES

Cocktails
"MEAN REDS"
(A spicy Manhattan cocktail)

2 ounces Maker's Mark bourbon
1 ounce sweet red vermouth
2 dashes Angostura bitters
1 drop Dave's Total Insanity hot sauce, or Tabasco to taste

Mix the ingredients together in a cocktail shaker filled with ice. Shake well and pour into chilled cocktail glasses. Garnish with a twist of orange peel.

Drink up. Laugh bitterly. Wipe mascara that has run down your cheek in rivulets of tears.

A PERFECT MARTINI

2 ounces Hendricks gin
1 small splash dry vermouth
2 dashes orange bitters

Mix in a cocktail shaker filled with ice. Shake languidly and pour into chilled glasses. Garnish with two olives.

Sip indolently. Express amusement with gay, tinkling laughter. Name your olives, then eat them.

JOE BELL'S WHITE ANGEL

2 ounces Bombay Sapphire gin
1 ounce Triple Sec
2 ounces grapefruit juice

Mix in a cocktail shaker filled with ice. Shake vigorously and pour into a chilled cocktail glass. Garnish with a slice of white grapefruit.

Polish off in two gulps. Toss head back and laugh wildly, desperately. Place lampshade on head, dance. Collapse in regret. Pour dividend.

Entrée

CHUTNEY MEATLOAF

1 pound ground beef
1 pound sweet Italian pork sausage
2 eggs
½ cup dried bread crumbs
1 onion, minced
1 red bell pepper, chopped
2 tbsp ketchup
1 tbsp salt
1 tbsp ground pepper
1 tsp cinnamon
1 small jar Major Grey or Mango Chutney

Preheat the oven to 350°F. In a large bowl, mix all the ingredients but the chutney. Do not overmix. Pack the meat mixture (not too tightly) into a loaf pan, and top with a nice layer of chutney. Bake for 1½ hours.

SERVES 6

SALLY TOMATOES

4 cups cherry tomatoes
3 to 4 tbsp extra-virgin olive oil
Salt and freshly ground black pepper
1 cup chopped fresh basil

Preheat the oven to 500°F. Place the tomatoes in a single layer on baking sheet with sides, toss with olive oil, salt, and pepper and roast for 10 to 15 minutes, or until slightly melted. Put the melted tomatoes in a bowl and toss with the basil.

SERVES 6

POTATOES GOLIGHTLY

6 to 8 Yukon Gold potatoes, cut into chunks
8 garlic cloves, left in their skins
1 onion, cut into chunks
4 small turnips, cut into small chunks
2 to 4 tbsp extra-virgin olive oil
Salt and freshly ground black pepper to taste

Preheat the oven to 450°F. Place the potatoes, garlic, and onion in a cast-iron pan. Place the turnips in a smaller baking pan. Toss both the potatoes and turnips with a little olive oil, salt, and pepper, and place both into the oven to roast. Check after 25 to 30 minutes; the potatoes will probably be done, but the turnips may need 5 to 10 more minutes. Remove the turnips when soft and golden. Toss the potato mixture with the turnips. May be served warm or at room temperature.

SERVES 6

LULAMAE'S BRIAR PATCH SALAD

8 to 10 organic navel oranges
1 or 2 red onions, depending on how much you like red onions
1 cup oil-cured Moroccan olives
16 ounces of arugula
$\frac{1}{8}$ cup walnut oil or extra-virgin olive oil
3 tbsp red wine vinegar
Salt and lots of freshly ground black pepper to taste

Peel the navel oranges with a sharp knife and cut into bite-size chunks. Do this on a plate, because it's a very juicy process. As the plate fills up with juice, pour it into your salad bowl, along with the orange pieces. Cut the red onion in half, then cut into half-moon pieces, and add to the bowl. Add the arugula and olives and toss with the oil and vinegar. Add salt to taste, and be generous with the pepper.

SERVES 6

Dessert
RUSTY TRAWLER'S RAW BABY BUTTOCKS
(Vanilla Pear Pudding)

2 cans or jars (15-ounce) pears in light syrup

$\frac{1}{3}$ cup flour

$\frac{1}{8}$ cup sugar

1 cup vanilla yogurt (Stonyfield Farms is preferable)

2 eggs

1 tsp vanilla extract

1 tsp almond extract

3 tsp brown sugar

Preheat the oven to 375°F. Drain the pears, saving ½ to ¾ cup syrup, and cut into bite-size chunks. In a blender, or in a bowl with a hand-blender, mix the flour and sugar. Add the yogurt, eggs, vanilla and almond extracts, and pear syrup. Grease a pie plate or shallow baking dish. Arrange the pear pieces on the bottom of the dish and pour the batter over the pears. Sprinkle with brown sugar. Bake for 25 to 30 minutes, or until the center is set.

WOMEN AND WINE
TIPS FROM *MY* HOLLY GOLIGHTLY

MY FRIEND BETH VON BENZ IS A SOMMELIER IN NEW YORK City. She always has the best advice about wine, so I asked her some questions, which I thought would be a lot more interesting than reading a bunch of wine books and making stuff up. I have a lot of questions about wine, like, "Please explain why white zinfandel is even called 'wine' with a straight face," and "You drink a lot of wine for your job—any tips on how to avoid the dreaded red-wine hangover?" and "I would like to come live with you and do some in-depth research on what a New York sommelier eats and drinks over the course of a few weeks. Will your husband mind if I stay on your couch?"

I didn't get all of my questions answered, but she was kind enough to take a break from her whirlwind schedule of luncheons, tastings, La Paulee de New York, and other wine events long enough to give me some valuable advice for women who enjoy wine, who have an interest in wine, but who are perhaps secretly intimidated by the whole process of buying and enjoying.

"We are all able to embrace that new cell phone, car, DVD player, camera—read the manual, and conquer it in a matter of minutes. But highly educated, intelligent, sophisticated women go into a wine store and say . . . . . . ?? It's a man's world in much of the wine world," says Beth. "Yet women buy the most wine."

Beth should really be writing her own book, which I'm sure she'll do when she's tired of tasting wine in Greece and Portugal and Chile, and being invited to fabulous wine-tasting parties all the time.

As in almost every other area of life, the way to not be intimidated is to know something, even a little bit, about the subject. Knowledge is power. "If you drink wine and enjoy it, the best advice I have for you is to *remember* what you tasted. I realize this sounds difficult, but it can be mastered in the simplest way."

Beth suggests you make space in your BlackBerry or iPhone—or, for those of us who still don't have a BlackBerry or iPhone, perhaps a small, fetching notebook and a pen. When you're in a restaurant, if you're having a glass of wine and you like what you or a friend has ordered, you can write the name down. Or, if you've just had the house wine, or the waiter recommended a wine and you liked the taste of it, ask the waiter to write it down for you.

Beth is a firm believer in finding a wine shop that you like, near your house or your work. You may be saving money at the big box store, but if a lot of the wine you purchase ends up being awful, then it's not really a bargain. A nice wine store will offer personal service, and there's always someone there to give a good recommendation. For instance, there's a very enthusiastic guy at my favorite wine shop, Du Vin; once, when I was looking for a good rosé from Provence, he grabbed a bottle off the shelf and told me he'd drunk an entire bottle of it the day before, while vacuuming his house. The way he rhapsodized about this wine made vacuuming the house sound very romantic. It made me want to rush home and start vacuuming immediately. Or at least rush home and drink some of that wine.

Beth also suggests that you find a wine store that does lots of wine tastings, so you can take notes, compare, and see what you like. "Eventually you'll be able to help them custom-make your wine order for you. That's their job."

"When I worked in a wine store, a woman once came in and said, 'I had this great bottle of chardonnay and I can't remember the name, but it had a white label and gold writing.' You need to stop yourself from ever saying anything like that. This can be avoided by paying a bit of attention and by taking notes. The more serious *you* are the more serious the person helping you will be.

"As an example, in a restaurant you might say, 'I'm having the roast chicken, but I like a red wine that's smooth and juicy.' The sommelier will probably give you a pinot noir from California or Oregon." So, use language that will help you get your point across.

Here are some more helpful tips from Beth:

- Don't box yourself into a corner. Try new wines, grape varieties, countries, styles. Be adventurous. In this economy, the wackier, more obscure the wine, the less it costs. Supply and demand, very simple.

- No one is an expert. The world of wine is vast, and changes very quickly. Vintages can be drastically different, the hardworking father dies and the son takes over the business and buys a Ferrari and doesn't give a hoot about the family's reputation, all kinds of things happen.

- Don't be afraid to speak up and ask questions. This is easier if you do some homework first. A great beginner's wine book is the paperback *Wine for Dummies* written by a very talented woman. It starts out at a beginner's level and before you know it you're hooked.

- Start having fun! When you go out to restaurants, make a point of talking to the waiter or sommelier. Find a wine person in your favorite retail store. Lots of stores keep track of what you buy, and with your notes you can go far in a short period of time.

- Throw a party, or organize a dinner with some wine friends. Take a wine course, or go to a wine tasting with your loved one.

She also has some gentle hints to help you along the way:

- Never talk about the "legs" of a wine. Anyone who does is a bonehead.

- When swirling your glass, always keep the glass on the table or surface it's on, don't try to swirl while standing at a party!

- Your taste might differ from your husband's, boyfriend's, girlfriend's, or that of a famed wine magazine. That does not mean you are wrong. Wine is a matter of personal taste. If you love the Trader Joe's $3.00 chardonnay, more power to you!

- Enjoy yourself! It should be a fun experience. The wine profession is sometimes taken so seriously. And keep your mind open . . . try a rosé wine or Greek wine. Live dangerously!

So, every single time you have a sip, taste, glass, or bottle of wine, make a quick note. Try to make a quick note even when you're at a party. Do I like this? Why do I like it? Do I think it's too rich? Too oak-y? Too fruity or sweet, too heavy, too light, too tannic, too juicy, or too boring? Someone may wonder why you are jotting down notes at a party, or what your notes are about. Is she making a note about my hairstyle? Is she jotting down that conversation I just had about my friend's affair? It will be a great icebreaker, and as soon as your fellow partygoers realize you aren't writing a commentary on the peculiar way they dance, they will probably want to hear your thoughts on wine, and what you've learned so far. Maybe they'll have some interesting knowledge to share with you.

"Just like learning a language," says Beth, "you can't take a pill or just listen to a tape and start speaking fluently, you have to work on it. Really, I would rather practice tasting wine any day than memorize irregular verbs in Spanish, right?"

I still don't know the answer to my question about white zinfandel, or whether Beth is, at this moment, arranging for me to accompany her on a series of fabulous wine-tasting jaunts while she makes up a bed for me on her sofa, but I think I've got a good start on my wine education. Thanks, Beth!

HERE'S HOW YOU DO IT:
IT'S A PARTY!!

YOU WANT TO CELEBRATE SPRING! OR SUMMER, OR FALL, OR winter. You want to celebrate your new shoes, you want to celebrate the fact that the sun came up. The point is, you just want to get a bunch of friends together, eat and drink, and whoop it up. But the thought of actually throwing that party is almost too much to bear. All you can think of is the work of cooking food for all those people, or the cost of catering and booze. The most vivid picture that comes to mind is you, with sore party feet, washing dishes at two A.M. Suddenly the idea of a party just sounds like a lot of trouble.

But actually throwing a party doesn't have to be all that difficult, and there are ways to make it simpler. If you haven't hosted a party for a long, long time, then I say it's high time you had one. A cocktail soirée, a dinner party, or a big blowout shindig—parties are fun! You may have forgotten, but they are such a blast. At least the good ones are. So how do you make your party one of those fabled "good ones"?

Invite an interesting mix of nice people. Have enough to

drink and enough to eat; maybe a little music in the background, to make it festive to the ears. It's that simple. You can get more or less elaborate, depending on how much energy you've got. If you want to do less and keep it homey, skip the caterer and hire your friend's fabulous daughter, or a local student who might want to make a little extra scratch. Hiring a helper will free you up to do any food preparation you might want to do, and will enable you to get yourself ready before the party starts; your wonderful helper can wipe down glasses, set up the buffet, and generally make him- or herself useful while you dress and primp, especially if you have your fabulous helper come in an hour or two before the party starts. Depending on how big the party is and how many drinkers you've invited, think about hiring a bartender for a few hours, so you're not stuck behind the bar for hours at your own party, just because you've got a reputation for making a perfect martini, for instance. I'm just saying, it could happen.

But the important part about having a party, and why we should have them more often, is to gather groups of friends together. It's about sitting down with people you love and mentally putting your feet up. It's about making a small celebration, possibly for no reason, but just because you enjoy the company and conversation of interesting people. You can talk politics, or have a sing-along, depending on the group you've invited; you can taste wines, discuss books, stay up late and watch old movies. You can feed them all dinner or have a potluck. You can have a summer picnic, a formal dress-up party, a costume party, a pajama party, an elegant cocktail party, or a last-minute let's-grab-a-pizza party. The point is, we know some great people, and it's really fun getting together with them, isn't it? We should really do it more often.

TIME FOR PARTY SNACKS!

With very little effort and a huge reward, you can make the following quick pickles as a delicious accompaniment to a simple poached salmon or roast chicken. A vat of delicious Mexican beans, a chopped salad with salsa dressing on the side, a nice, bright Sauvignon Blanc, and you've got yourself a top-shelf party meal.

Treat yourself to some delicious . . .
QUICK SPICY PICKLED ONIONS

These quick pickles are not only a fantastic side dish for Mexican food; they make a delightfully piquant appetizer when friends stop by for cocktails.

2 cups apple cider vinegar

¼ cup plus 1 tsp sugar

2 tsp dried oregano

1 tsp salt

Pinch of ground cumin

1 tbsp extra-virgin olive oil

5 onions, a combination of red, Vidalia, and white

3 fresh jalapeños, sliced

Combine the vinegar, the ¼ cup sugar, the oregano, salt, cumin, and ½ cup water in a medium saucepan over medium heat. Bring the mixture to a simmer while you prepare the onions. Peel the onions, cut them in half from root to stem, then thinly slice each half into half-moons.

Heat the oil in a heavy-bottomed pan over high heat and sauté the onions and jalapeños with the remaining teaspoon of sugar for just a few minutes.

Pour the hot brine mixture over the onions. As soon as it comes to a slow simmer, remove from the heat and let sit, covered, for 15 minutes. Transfer the onions, jalapeños, and brine into clean jars with tight-fitting lids and refrigerate. These quick pickles are ready to eat as soon as they're cold, and will keep in the fridge for up to 2 weeks. If they last that long.

Or perhaps a handful of tasty quick-pickled vegetables
SPICY PICKLED VEGETABLES

- 4 tsp kosher salt
- 1 tsp ground cumin
- 2 pounds baby carrots
- 2 cups pearl onions, peeled, or sliced red onion
- 2 large sliced jalapeños
- 2 cups trimmed haricots verts (thin French green beans)
- 4 cups white vinegar

In a large saucepan, bring the salt, cumin, and 6 cups water to a boil over medium-high heat. Add the carrots and cook 2 minutes. Add the onions and cook 1 minute. Add the jalapeños and cook 1 minute. Add the haricots verts and cook 1 minute. Remove from the heat and stir in the vinegar. Let stand at room temperature 1 hour.

Pour the mixture into a large bowl, cover, and refrigerate 24 hours. Store in an airtight container in the refrigerator for up to 2 weeks.

EASY POACHED SALMON

A poached salmon is one of the easiest things you can make for a party. Try to get wild salmon rather than farmed; it's more flavorful and you'll be more supportive of the environment. If you're having a big party, see if you can get a deal on a half or whole salmon. For a smaller party, you can buy individual pieces and poach them in batches.

The poaching broth can be as simple or as complicated as you want to make it. Water, a splash of dry vermouth, a bay leaf, some sliced onion and garlic; or use vegetable or chicken broth with white wine, fresh dill, and minced garlic. But the basic recipe is this:

Fill a large pot with cold water, add a cup of white wine, a bay leaf, some peppercorns, a handful of minced garlic and onion, a handful of thyme or tarragon. Bring this to a boil, then gently drop your salmon pieces into the pot with a spatula. Make sure the fish is completely covered in liquid, cover the pot, and turn off the heat. Let sit for exactly 30 minutes, then gently remove the salmon with a slotted spatula, place on a plate, and cool. The salmon will be moist and delectable; you may eat it warm or chilled. Serve with a dollop of peppered mayonnaise. Play around with the mayonnaise sauce: add a little mustard, add some spicy Thai Sriracha sauce, or add a little low-fat yogurt and a handful of chopped dill for a lighter sauce.

You can cut the salmon into smaller chunks for a party, and serve with a bowl of sauce your guests can ladle over their fish. Or, you can break up the salmon into pieces, toss with lemon juice, olive oil, and some of your mayonnaise sauce. Serve over a bed of arugula.

With fresh salsa and fresh tortillas, your guests can make their own little salmon tacos at the table, using the spicy fresh pickles as a topping or a side dish. Oh, YUM.

IN PRAISE OF A GOOD COCKTAIL

IF I HAVE SAID IT ONCE, I HAVE SAID IT A THOUSAND TIMES: There is no such thing, thankfully, as a "light" martini. As in, "Ooh, I've never had a martini. Could you make me a light one?" You either have a martini, or you don't have a martini. You can have a sip of someone else's martini, if you don't think you can handle your own. But if you want a "light" martini, order a gin and tonic. Drinking is a little like skiing, in that no one needs to know you're a beginner if you pretend you know what you're doing. So if you've never gotten the hang of having a drink once in a while, don't make a big deal of it. Don't exclaim like an ex-Mormon sneaking her first cappuccino. Watch a few *Thin Man* movies and pretend you're Myrna Loy.

Perhaps in your youth you had an unfortunate experience with a Tequila Sunrise, or sloe gin and 7Up. You think of your forays into drinking as youthful high jinks, and so now you only occasionally sip chardonnay with the girls. You assert that you've tried something called a Lemon Drop, and could I make you one of those? No, I'm afraid I draw the line at anything involving large amounts of corn syrup and flavorings, because I know you will feel just awful in the morning. I'm not encouraging you to down a fifth of whiskey every morning, but we've reached an age where we ought to be able to mix a few martinis for friends who drop by in the evening without it being some kind of special event.

I've always been under the impression that drinking was meant to be a fun thing to do. For years I've been extolling the virtues of the mighty martini, the ice-cold goodness of a martini, a real martini, made with gin. A martini, with a sliver of lemon or a briny olive; a Gibson with a pickled onion. For years, I have felt like the lone drunk in the wilderness. That is, until I read the highly entertaining book by Barbara Holland, *The Joy of Drinking*. You'll be captivated by the depth of her historical research and delighted by her wit and insight. It's chock-full of an infinite variety of drinking lore, obscure information, and nuggets of wisdom, such as the fact that there are "no good milk-drinking songs."

I will be giving a copy to my father, an unapologetic martini drinker, who has been known to make waiters squirm when he orders his martini and they innocently ask, "Gin or vodka?" His reaction is unfailingly entertaining. You do not want to be on the other end of that conversation.

That said, some of us are not the drinkers we once were, nor do we wish to necessarily be the drinkers we once were. We find that the day following a particularly exuberant evening of alcohol-fueled festivity is no longer a matter of a few aspirin and a cup of coffee. The results of "overdoing it" are closer to the symptoms of a rare strain of Asian flu than a simple hangover. Somehow, as we age, having "a few too many" ends up making us feel as if we have injected pure ethyl alcohol into our frontal lobes. With a rusty needle. The kind used to inject bears. The entire day is pretty much shot. Lying down and making moaning noises must be alternated with swallowing handfuls of aspirin washed down with tomato juice. Followed by a banana. And a cold washcloth on your forehead. And another go at lying down. And more weak-but-fervent moaning.

A simple hangover is no longer all that simple. In order to avoid this sad and painful state of affairs, we need to once again keep balance in mind. I just love having a cold cocktail with friends. Sometimes two. I have been known to share an entire bottle of wine with a single person. But the best outcome for the following day is when that bottle of wine is shared over the course of an entire evening, with a few glasses of water in between, and of course, some food to cushion the blow. So let's be grown-up about our cocktails, and take our milk thistle supplements and get enough water and potassium, and know when to stop drinking during the course of the evening.

And a few little preventive tips:

• If it's green, pink, or sports a colorful umbrella and/
or plastic monkey, or arrives in a large football-shaped
object, chances are you will be feeling less than your
stellar self in the morning.

• Avoid overloading yourself with the brown spirits
(bourbon, scotch), which are lovely for sipping,
but not so lovely for an entire evening of joyful

carousing. Stick with the clear ones (gin, vodka) if you know you're going to make an evening of it, or if you're involved in some sort of political drinking game.

- Whatever you do, don't follow too many of either with a lot of red wine. Trust me on this. In case you haven't already felt the remarkably horrible effects of this combination, I urge you not to try. Just for future reference, it's like a hangover times a hundred. A hangover cubed to the ninth power. A *Matrix* hangover, reloaded. It will make you want to scoop your eyes out with a melon-baller. So try not to do it accidentally, in the excitement of the moment.

- And do raise your glass in a toast as often as possible. Toast to everyone's health, toast to happiness and good fortune, toast to Bacchus and Dionysus, toast to love and friendship. (And offer anyone a bed who might need one.)

IT'S NOT CASUAL FRIDAY. IT'S A PARTY

LADIES, WE'RE GOING TO A PARTY, NOT THE GROCERY STORE. We're not dressing for a meeting at the office, or to volunteer at the school canned-goods drive. It's a party. That means dressing "up." Dressing down is what you do when you're taking your car into the shop, or getting ready to ride your bike through a sketchy neighborhood, or getting ready for a walk on the beach. What is this aversion so many women seem to have for getting dolled up? Yes, I know, you might feel out of place showing up to the local library fund-raising party in one of those dramatic ensembles pulled from the runways at fashion week. It might be impractical to walk over to Joanne's potluck in a pair of six-inch Louboutins, and it's not always possible to fit that giant head-dress of twigs and tulle into your average-size late-model sedan. You might feel ridiculous wearing sequins and drag makeup to your neighbor's wine 'n' cheese party, and I certainly don't want any of us to feel ridiculous. But that's no reason for us to just fall back on elastic-waist denim and an old sweatshirt. We're grown-up women, and just because we're over forty doesn't mean we have to blend in. Surely we can raise the stakes a tiny bit? The ubiquitous khaki slacks, the "California casual" garb so favored by women over a certain age? Where's the kick? Where's the style? Where's the imagination? Where are the slim black capris and the orange leather mules? You get this one life, and, sadly, only a limited number of parties to which you will be invited. So why not dress up? It's a party. You won't stick out like a sore thumb if you look more elegant than the assembled guests. Perhaps they will look down at their casual-Friday pants and rethink their party attire next time they have an opportunity.

If you're not used to getting gussied up, then start with baby steps. Start thinking about dressing up in a different way. Just take it up a dressy little notch. You don't have to pile on the jewels and the chiffon and the updo and the tippy heels all at the same time. But there's some fun to be mined there. You don't have to make a big deal about it; it shouldn't be a big deal when you get dressed up. It should be just one more opportunity to enjoy your bad self. Bask in it a little. Relish your red shantung silk cocktail dress and gold mules, or that low-backed number with a pair of fishnet stockings. If you've never worn a little black dress, then maybe it's time to make one a part of your wardrobe. Maybe wearing that little black dress to the grocery store once in a while would give you a small boost. If wearing black dresses is your way of blending in, then perhaps it's time to add a little color to the mix. Start looking for occasions to dress up. Express your delightful personality with your style. Dress up for fun, because maybe it'll make you feel spectacular. Have a party, because dressing up is a great excuse to have a party.

IN FACT, EVERY WOMAN
NEEDS A BALL GOWN

If not now, when? Have you ever owned a ball gown, not counting the one you made out of a hand-me-down petticoat when you were six years old? If you have, I think that's soooo dreamy, and I want to know if it has yards of silk chiffon, or a train, or a tulle petticoat. Or maybe it's made entirely of silk tulle, and when you enter a room you sort of waft, like a cloud of perfume.

I think we've reached an age where we've earned a ball gown. And I think once you have your ball gown, you should just start wearing it to dinner parties and when you're going to have drinks at a friend's house. Because, unless you're a foreign dignitary or a real princess or a movie star, no one is inviting us to any balls. (Or maybe it's just me. If it is, I'm fine about it, really! You go and have fun, honestly, I was busy anyway.) But why should movie stars have all the fun? What if I didn't go to foreign dignitary school? Does that mean no ball gown for me, ever? That just doesn't seem fair.

So it's time to get a ball gown. And I think that once you start wearing your ball gown out to parties, people will start thinking to themselves, "Hey, how come I always wear these jeans to parties? I know they cost $600, but damn, they're jeans! What was I thinking, wearing jeans to a party? Ball gowns are so pretty and frothy, I wish I had a ball gown. In fact, why don't people start having dressy parties again? I think I'll throw a really dressy party right away, with cocktails and hors d'oeuvres! And the first person I invite will be that striking woman over there in that fantastic ball gown!"

E-Z
*Ballerina
Cocktail
Frock*

THIS PART fits on top just above your strapless bra

tie sash around your middle

sew and gather

elastic

cut hem to desired length
the cut end becomes your sash

First, if you don't have a sewing machine, find a friend with a sewing machine. Preferably a friend like Geri, who is the kind of person you can call up at eight P.M. the night before a party and ask if she wouldn't mind helping you to "sew a seam." "Sewing a seam" really means "arriving with two different pieces of fabric and two different ideas for two different dresses, and only a vague idea of how to put them together." Which I actually did, the night before a big party, not long ago. Sure, I could have *bought* a dress, but that would be taking the easy way out. Anyone can just *buy* a dress. And sometimes a girl has a vision. It was perhaps foolhardy to have this kind of vision the night before a party. But boy, was it fun! Geri and I figured the whole thing out, and she helped me make two dresses in about two hours, while adding amusing commentary on the nun who taught her to sew, and how she'd be spinning in her grave. Both styles are pretty easy to put together, and each style is bound to look good on somebody.

If you have a good imagination, the Ballerina Cocktail dress is a charming combination of a 1948 Christian Dior New Look gown and a costume worn by a down-at-the-heels carnival tight-rope walker in a formerly grand Eastern Bloc circus.

For your Ballerina Cocktail Frock, you will need:

- One long or medium-length pink or black tutu (available at Capezio or other dance supply shop)

- A length of lightweight silk, at least two yards (but the more fabric, the fuller your skirt)

- A strip of one-inch-wide elastic long enough to fit
  around your chest

- A sturdy strapless bra

Measure your elastic so it fits around your chest comfortably, just where the top of a strapless dress would hit.

Gather your fabric so it fits on the length of elastic; either sew a channel and slide your elastic through the panel, or fold the fabric over the elastic and sew it directly. You should now have a large, tent-like silk skirt.

Place your tutu low on your hips. Pull your tent-like skirt over your head and let it sit just above your strapless bra. To get the length right, cinch in the fabric at your waist with a belt or a scarf, and cut the length of your strapless dress to just above the bottom edge of your tutu. Use that cut-off fabric as your sash. I like the bottom edge to be slightly uneven, so it's a little shorter in front and longer in back, so the tutu shows a bit at the bottom. When the length is to your liking, sew up the back seam. Cinch yourself tightly around your waist with your sash and adjust accordingly. Instant Ballerina Cocktail Frock!

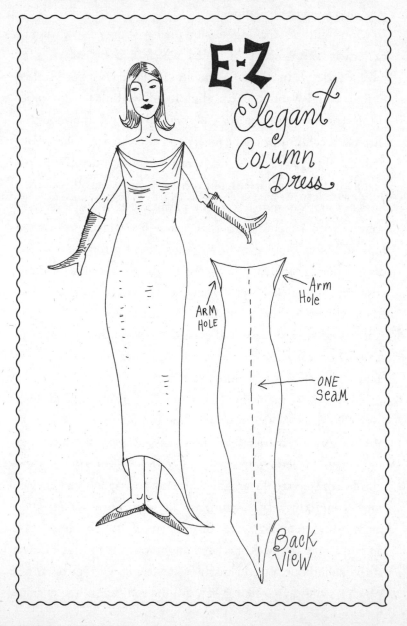

E-Z

Elegant

Column

Dress

ARM
HOLE

Arm
Hole

ONE
SEAM

Back
View

You will need 1 to 1¼ yards of stretchy knit fabric, safety pins, and a sewing machine.

You will be making a slim-fitting (but not skintight), extremely simple column dress, which can be strapless or have a wide boatneck and armholes. Because it's a very simple design, you'll want to find a slightly nubby knit fabric, something stretchy, with texture and interest and color, although a slim black column would be lovely, too. Measure the fabric from your shoulders to the floor, and wrap it around yourself approximately to fit. Have a friend pin the dress on you, as if you are a human tailor's dummy. You'll be pinning essentially a straight column with a slight hourglass shape; a little bigger around the hips and bust, nipping in at the waist, the bottom part of the dress tapering smaller down your thighs to your knees. Once your line is pinned, carefully wiggle out of the dress and sew the seam; the "right side" of the fabric facing the right side of the fabric, so the sewn seam will eventually be on the inside of the dress. Do not sew the entire length of the column; sew the seam to just below where your knees will be.

When the seam is sewn, turn the fabric inside out and slip it over your head. Notice your arms are pinned to your sides. Oh no! But wait. Your friend will now take her very sharp scissors and cut slits where your arms will go. Stick your arms out the slits and make sure the armholes are not too tight. Once they're cut to your liking, sew around the edges of the armholes to keep them from stretching wider or unraveling. Put the dress back on and check the neckline. You might want it to drape down at the collarbone, or you might want to cut a wider opening. When it's cut to your liking, sew around the edge of the neck to finish. Help your friend as best as you can, even if you're totally hopeless with scissors and a needle. Put the dress on again and check the length. Cut the bottom to just above the ankles in front, and longer in back, to give you a "fishtail" hem. You can leave the bottom edge unfinished, or sew the edges for a more finished look. Instant Elegant Column Dress! At this point you must open a bottle of wine and pour your friend a large glass of it, if you haven't done so already. Toast to the joy of a new frock, to your good friend, and to your mutual ingenuity!

YOU CAN MAKE IT YOURSELF!
THE BEST GIFT ON A SMALL BUDGET

HERE IS A GIFT THAT IS EASY FOR ANYONE TO MAKE, FOR those times when you're feeling financially pinched or when you have no idea what to get your friend for her birthday, because she already has everything anyone could possibly want. All you need is a good X-Acto knife, a hardcover book, some glue, and a swatch of fabric. I first made this gift for a boy who was turning twelve, and have since made it for other young gents, including my two sons, and a few girlfriends. It's always a tremendous hit. Who in the world would not love to have their very own secret treasure box, disguised as a book?

So here's what you do: go to the bookstore and see if you can find one of those hardcover reissues of the *Hardy Boys* or *Nancy Drew* books. Buy the whole set, if you can swing it; that way you'll be able to make this gift whenever you're pressed for time.

It's not necessary to purchase a brand-new book; you can also go to a used bookstore and find any sturdy hardcover book. Find something that looks dusty and mysterious, or a book that looks completely idiotic: a dated textbook would be a fun choice, or an old-fashioned mystery. It should have a reasonable thickness; the thicker the better.

Open the book to a few pages or a few chapters in, perhaps at the beginning of an exciting-sounding chapter heading. You're going to carve out a rectangular hole in your book, which you will then line with a swatch of velvet, or brocade, or Astroturf, or any fabric of your choice. Depending on the size of the book, use an index card or a postcard as your template by tracing a line around the outer edge of your template onto the page in your book where you've decided to position the secret hiding place. If you can't find an appropriate template, simply measure and draw a square or rectangle shape, using a ruler. You'll want to keep a margin of at least an inch around your square or rectangle.

Take your X-Acto blade, and, holding the pages closed, start carving into the pages, following the line of your template. Your blade should be extremely sharp so as to not rip the pages. The inside of your square doesn't matter so much, because you'll be discarding that portion. But you want to keep the lines as neat as possible, so that the sides of the eventual "box" are fairly uniform.

It is a bit of a process to cut through the layers of paper, so you'll be cutting through a layer of maybe fifteen pages at a time. When you find yourself getting close to the back cover, put down a piece of cardboard or something, so you don't slice right through the back. Once you've sliced through the book up to the back cover and have cut out your compartment, you'll need to carefully glue the loose pages together to form a solid block. The best way to apply the glue is with a brush, so the paper doesn't bunch up. You also want to have a light hand with the glue, so it doesn't start seeping out of the outside edges and make a big mess. If it does seep out, just take your finger or brush and brush it in. Glue the pages in layers, and hold the book closed in between gluing. Every single page does not have to be glued together: after this, you will apply glue to the inner walls of your secret hidey-hole and to the bottom of the compartment, which you will line with your swatch of fabric. Shut the book and put something weighty on top so it will dry solid. (Place a piece of fabric across the top page of the compartment, to keep any stray glue from gluing the whole book closed.)

After about an hour, open the book and remove your place-holder fabric. You should have a perfectly lovely, solidly glued, fabric-lined secret hiding place carved into the book. At this point, you may decide you want to decorate the inner cache a little more elaborately. You can paint the "walls" of the stash box in a solid color, or glue more fabric along the sides. You can write secret messages around the top of the cache-hole, or glue photographs of you and the recipient on the margins of the compartment. Don't overdo it, though—you want the book to be able to close properly.

Fill it with a few treasures, like a couple of gold coins, or a bookstore gift certificate, dice, a special rock, some chocolate, a small deck of cards, a bracelet, a monocle, a tiny set of colored pencils—whatever fits. Tie it with a beautiful ribbon. It should look like an ordinary book from the outside, but then your friend will open it, and find the secret compartment, and the hidden treasures, and she will be positively delighted. It is the BEST PRESENT EVER.

But now that you know how to make one, why not make yourself a secret book treasure box? I'll bet you've got a few old *Bobbsey Twins* or *Nancy Drew* volumes collecting dust on your shelf. Give yourself a cunning hiding place for your jewelry or a lovely keepsake box while giving new life to an old book. Unless it's a valuable first edition, of course. Or you still like to curl up with *Nancy Drew* from time to time, which sounds like a pretty comfy thing to do on a lazy Sunday.

OTHER HOMEMADE GIFTS ON A SHOESTRING BUDGET

- Type up five or ten of your favorite recipes and decorate the typed pages—photos, a finger painting, a drawing of the dish in question. Have each recipe laminated. Or collect a menu's worth of recipes. Make a cover, if you want, where you print out "Marge's Birthday Dinner Menu" or "Janet's Favorite Soups" or "Hors d'Oeuvres for the Holidays" or "Cocktails for Professional Drinkers" or what have you. Laminate the cover, too. Line up the cover and the laminated pages and punch three holes on the left side, or just one hole in the top left corner. Tie the pages together with brads or ribbons.

- Invent a cocktail and name it after a friend you wish to honor. You may then mix your friend his or her eponymous cocktail on a special evening, as you present this lucky friend with a copy of the custom recipe. If you are feeling especially flush, gather together the cocktail's various ingredients and arrange them together in a basket, along with a couple of cocktail glasses, a shaker (if the recipe calls for a shaker), and a laminated copy of the cocktail recipe.

THE MONA LISA
Created for my friend Lisa,
who is not a big drinker.

Campari
The juice of 1 orange or tangerine
Plain sparkling soda
Orangina
Slice of orange for garnish

Fill a tall highball glass with ice.
Add 1 ounce Campari and the orange or tangerine juice. Fill the rest of the glass with equal parts soda and Orangina, to taste. Stir, and garnish with a slice of orange. Enjoy! Then put down your cocktail and help Ryder with his LEGO pirate ship. Try not to leave your cocktail sitting on the bureau for a half hour while the ice melts.

Cheers!

PLAY!

FOR THE PAST FEW BIRTHDAYS, MY OLD FRIEND MICHAEL ARATA has been sending me the greatest present: one of those old Pin the Tail on the Donkey games*, with the tails and blindfold attached, the kind that used to be a staple of children's birthday parties in the 1960s and 1970s. But since he's an artist, he takes the basic donkey picture and spells out:

Always Remember: Do Not Forget to Party

in different-colored rubber-stamp letters. As Michael says, "If you're blindfolded with a pin in your hand in the middle of a party, you know you're having fun!"

I have a few of these donkeys on my wall, because they're a good and constant reminder that we really ought to make merry more often. When I stop in front of the donkey and read those words, it will often give me just the little reminder I need to con-

---

*(Order your own! They're not easy to find, but I found a supplier at American Carnival Mart. Google it!)

tinue the day with a livelier step. The little donkey is telling me to jump, or dance, put some flowers out, or light some candles. And when the little donkey speaks, we must listen. Everyone should have their own little donkey! We salute you, little donkey!

DO NOT FORGET TO PARTY!

A BREAK WITH BARBIE AND BETSY

Just as I think weekly massages should be subsidized by the government as a part of a comprehensive preventive health plan, my friend Wendy thinks that "Barbie breaks" should be an option for all working women. To alleviate on-the-job stress, she suggests that for fifteen minutes to a half hour every workday, the doors to offices around the country should close, in order to facilitate group Barbie breaks.

Women would gather with their Barbies, outfits, and accessories, and play Barbies, just as we did when we were younger. Doors to executive offices would close for the Barbie break. CEOs and CFOs would unfold Barbie wardrobes, and tiny shoe collections would be retrieved from file cabinets. It would be a chance to relax, to unwind, to work out your personal and workplace problems, and, of course, to live vicariously through your Barbie as you dress her up in her black-sequined evening gown or her astronaut togs. Instead of the traditional pint of bourbon in the bottom drawer, we could have our Midges and Skippers.

Likewise, I think paper-doll breaks are also an excellent idea. Remember Betsy McCall? Wouldn't it be great if we could have a grown-up Betsy McCall, with new outfits and hairdos arriving to our inbox every week? And making your own paper-doll outfits simply cannot be overestimated as a creative outlet. Simply place a piece of paper over your doll and trace her outline. Then create a stunning fashion ensemble of your own! The meditative and therapeutic qualities that come from the regular cutting out of paper dolls and their attendant outfits will get you through the rest of the workday, and perhaps give you some creative ideas for your own wardrobe when you make your weekend plans.

GAMES LEARNED FROM
ELEVEN-YEAR-OLD BOYS

Yes, we're girls, albeit girls who've been around the block a few times. We're girls, but sometimes we can get some good ideas from the boys. Why? Because we all need to channel our inner eleven-year-old boy from time to time. Because sometimes you just need to go with a good idea. Because, come on, farts are funny. They're funny, right?

Okay, and so are butts, apparently. So next time you're in the car with a friend, or friends, play the butt game! A game invented by my bright, thoughtful eleven-year-old son. I am so proud.

Here's how to play. It's butt-simple. Merely substitute the word "butt" for words you see on billboards and restaurant signs, with street names and titles on movie posters. For instance, "Primrose Lane" cleverly turns into "Primrose Butt." See how much fun this game could add to your life? See how this might never get old? "Post No Butts" is just one of the many brilliant juxtapositions over which you and your friends will be in stitches. Car trips whiz by; you will effortlessly arrive at your destination having laughed, guffawed, chuckled, and groaned. Definitely groaned.

HENRY'S ACCORDION JOKE:
A HUMOR LITMUS TEST

My good friend Henry, who happens to play the accordion, told us this joke, and now my friend Peter uses it as his all-purpose litmus test for humor. If you don't laugh at this joke, Peter will then know that you don't have a sense of humor. Or maybe you just don't share his particular brand of humor. Or maybe you're just a very sensitive accordionist.

A musician is late for an appointment, so he pulls into a

parking place, locks the car, and races to his meeting, leaving his accordion in the backseat of his car.

When he returns, he finds that the backseat window has been broken. Someone broke into his car! Shocked and upset, he looks through the smashed window into the backseat of the car.

And sees two accordions.

The End.

SPEAKING OF HATS, AGAIN: YOUR FESTIVE PARTY HAT

I am a big fan of the Ditty Bops, and if you haven't heard any beautiful music in a while, you should just stop reading this minute and go get the Ditty Bops CD. The Ditty Bops are two beautiful and talented women who not only sing like angels, they do things like ride from Los Angeles to New York on their *bicycles*. Their music is delightful, and they are simply dreamy. Well, I had forgotten how cute a well-constructed paper crown could be until I saw Abby—who is adorable, but not preciously so—sporting one at a Ditty Bop concert. A lovely paper crown, the kind where you measure a band of construction paper around your head, tape it to fit, and then add feathers or tissue-paper flowers for decoration. I'm telling you, a good paper crown just screams "FUN." It announces to the room, "I am sitting on the head of a happy, confident woman, the kind of self-possessed gal who is not afraid to wear a construction-paper crown as an actual part of her wardrobe, without any smirking irony. So there! Now, where's the party punch? We'd like to cut a rug."

Maybe you're headed to a party and you feel as if your ensemble is missing that certain *je ne sais quoi*. A velvet cloak? A walking stick? A jaunty ascot? Perhaps you are missing that certain something that can only come from handmade preschool headgear. So keep some construction paper handy, make yourself a paper crown, and be queen for a day!

PART III

SO, HERE WE ARE

YOU, IN MIDLIFE: NOW WHAT?

I USED TO BE A SPY. I HAD ONLY A VAGUE RECOLLECTION OF THIS time in my life, until one day, when I found a mysterious envelope containing my former identification card, an encoded note, and a small journal. Inside the journal I found the key to the code, as well as a handful of brief descriptions of various "missions" I undertook with my friend and fellow spy Margaret.

If you have ever dreamed of being a spy, which apparently I did quite a bit when I was in seventh grade, you can finally attain that dream, as I did those many years ago. You've reached that time in your life when you might be ready for a little reinventing.

This suggestion to "become a spy" is not to denigrate my friend Amanda, who actually was a spy. A REAL spy. Once she was interrogated in a room for six hours. I think they might have even put a big hurt on her. You'd never guess from meeting Amanda that she was a real spy, because you could never imagine Amanda not talking to anybody. I mean "talking" in the sense of "spilling the beans." She's a delightfully hilarious, smart, and sometimes dizzy Brit who has a million stories of Swiss finishing school and her nutty Catholic mother. I didn't find out until years after I met her that she was *actually a spy*. I still don't know all the details; they're a little fuzzy. But I'm having lunch with her tomorrow, and I will torture her until she "talks." Perhaps by withholding the wine.

Okay. I got some more "intel." I swore I wouldn't use real names of the people she was spying *on* and stuff, but she was *really a spy*, and was really interrogated in a room for six hours. That is so cool! Okay, but wait until I tell you. Her "wire" malfunctioned or something. It stopped working! But she didn't know that! And her "contacts" were parked in a van outside, and couldn't hear her! She had to think really fast, but she also got a little cocky because she assumed her "contacts" were listening and had her back. Delicious!

Here are more things I found out, with very little coercion, really. It's amazing what people will tell you over a glass or two of wine. I don't think they tried that trick during Amanda's interrogation. They might have had better luck with her if they had. But she stayed mum. She didn't spill. She didn't sing like a canary. She had to do a lot of pretending, because she had a whole cover story she couldn't blow. What else?

• She had three identities. Three identities!

• One of her aliases was "Claire."

- She received her payment in cash, in an unmarked envelope. Which was handed to her. Just like in the movies!

- Someone may have been *murdered*.

- The man who originally hired her *disappeared* during the course of the investigation in which she was involved. My friend Amanda still doesn't know what happened to him. She speculated that he may have had to change his identity (change his identity!) for safety reasons, and go deeper undercover. She feared worse.

- She was a spy for three years. Three years!

The current Amanda is a mother of two daughters, and she cannot believe that she used to be a spy. Because, well, kind of dangerous and all. But if I were she, I would tell my daughters as soon as possible. Because, hello? "My mom was a spy?" There could not possibly be anything cooler than that.

The point is, perhaps you are looking for a little midlife change, the kind of change that doesn't involve hot flashes and liver spots. Well, just as we get to reinvent our fashion and makeup styles as often as we want, I believe we get to reinvent ourselves, too. As many times as it takes. I'm just saying, if you have always wanted to own a flower cart, be a mixologist, be a nude artist's model, start a catering company, be a landscape gardener, write a novel, learn to upholster furniture, design a line of clothing, hook a rug, be a court reporter, start a coffee roasting company, sell your famous relish, teach dance to children, or sail around the world, there is no time like the present. My friend Daniela took up the cello in her mid-forties, even though it often required her to play "Twinkle" variations with seven-year-olds. Five years later she's onto Bach concertos. My big sister let her hair go silver-white (which, oddly enough, took at least ten years off her face) and started taking ballet lessons and teaching art in an elementary school. My other sister won a spot in a fantastic writing program, is writing a novel, and plans to live in London and France with her new beau. So any one of us really can take up *plein air* painting and go live on a narrow boat on the canals of south Oxford.

My spying days may be over, and so may be Amanda's, but I have got a full list of things I think I'd like to at least try. Making your own list takes nothing more than a piece of paper, a pen, and your imagination. Aren't there a few things you've always wanted to do? Carry a small notebook around with you to write down ideas. Think about your dream goals before you go to sleep at night. See yourself actually doing all those things you imagine you'd like to do. In 1989, a fifty-six-year-old Illinois woman named Pat Henry started sailing singlehandedly around the world in a thirty-one-foot sailboat, financing the trip by selling watercolors she'd painted along the way. She was the first American woman—and the oldest woman—to ever complete a solo circumnavigation. "I began looking at how few women have made a voyage around the world alone," Pat Henry said, "and decided it would be a nice little club to join." Fifty-six years old! Twenty-nine hundred days alone at sea!

So go! Go find out how to get started. Learn what you've always wanted to learn, find out how to get the job or the life you've always wanted to have. The alone-at-sea part might not be your cup of tea, but if Pat Henry of Illinois can wake up one day and decide to sail around the world, surely you can figure out a way to have a job you love, or finally take that trip to Peru, or take surfing lessons.

Reinventing yourself doesn't mean you should suddenly adopt a phony British accent and join the circus. I think it's more about uncovering your authentic self; the finding out what your authentic self really wants to do and who she really is. It may not involve a daring adventure or a drastic change of scenery; your authentic self may be quite happy to avoid rogue waves in a thirty-one-foot sailboat. But you really should be doing what you love, don't you think? You may discover that your authentic self really likes being an accountant, or teacher, or lawyer, or artist. And if you discover that your authentic self prefers puttering around the garden, taking in a little sunshine, and figuring out what's for dinner, then try to do that as much as you possibly can.

IF YOU SHOULD ACTUALLY DECIDE TO BECOME A SPY

All you'll need is a Spy Kit, which can easily be assembled at home. In case you prefer a less dangerous line of work, a Detective Kit, which I created when I was nine or ten years old, may also easily be assembled in the comfort of your own home. Perhaps with a few trips to the thrift store and an office supply shop.

FOR THE SPY KIT

One dedicated Spy Journal

Your own written and oral secret code, which you will
create

Several aliases

Photo identification for each alias

Small flight bag

Assorted disguises

"Contact" number

Tiny cigarette lighter/camera (optional)

Proficiency in several foreign languages

FOR THE DETECTIVE KIT

One suitcase ("Private Eye" logo on exterior of case
optional, hand-drawn eye optional)

Written and oral secret code

Walkie-talkies (optional)

Assorted disguises and useful props and accessories,
which may consist of any or all of the following:

A variety of wigs

A small assortment of false mustaches and beards

A selection of easily packable hats

Eyeglasses, nonprescription, assortment of frame
styles

Sunglasses, assortment of frame styles

Trench coat (mandatory)

Gloves

You will also need a small, nondescript notebook or journal, in which you may jot down your thoughts and take notes while engaged in surveillance. Write in code when necessary.
Night goggles (optional)
A notepad, working pen

If you have found a job you love, and part of the reason you love it is because you work at home, then you are doubly lucky.

But: When You Work at Home, Don't Forget to Ring the Bell for Recess

OUR LESSER SELVES

So we've reached this age. This age, where we kind of expected that things would be, well, different. We thought that by now we'd have met a certain number of our own expectations. I mean, for heaven's sake, we've lived a ridiculous number of years and yet it feels like we're still working toward that magic pinnacle of achievement. It often seems frustratingly elusive, especially when those around us appear to be reaching it so easily. How do some people seem to lead such charmed lives? Why her, and not me? I know you know this, but I'm telling you again: your friend's successes are not your failures. Her shining career triumph doesn't mean you are by default a pathetic loser. Your successful friends have had fabulous success bombs fall on them, and one could fall on you, too! So celebrate all the successes in your life, including all the good things that befall your friends.

This is sometimes easier said than done. Especially when it seems so unfair that a particular "friend" not only had a giant success bomb fall on them, they have landed in a steaming pile of success, a soft, veritable dunghill of happy happy joy joy. You are worrying about how in the world you're going to pay next month's rent, and your friend

    a. gets paid more to "consult" two days a week than you, your parents, the Queen, and God have made in a lifetime

    b. enjoys a promotion, a large expense account, and having her house cleaned by someone else

    c. gets to take a vacation every year without having to save for it

    d. appears on magazine covers, which are often prominently displayed at the checkout of your local crappy supermarket where you stand in line at ten P.M. to pick up laundry detergent

You know you have talent; you have been waiting so patiently for that success bomb to fall, so you plaster a big smile on your face and make a dazzling attempt to be gracious when your friend starts to discuss her interior decorator and asks your opinion on her new nine-thousand-dollar loveseat. You've never seen a nine-thousand-dollar loveseat. You start thinking, bitterly, that she could have just paid you the nine thousand dollars and you would have found her a much cooler-looking loveseat at the thrift store. You start picking at old, scabby, acidic thoughts, and rubbing salt in them. But this is no way to live, and you know it.

It wreaks havoc on your complexion and your friendships.

Some friendships go through this sort of storm and fall by the wayside, which probably means they weren't the closest to begin with. But the good ones are so worth not screwing up just because you're bathing in envy and resentment. Just understand that no one's life is exactly what you think it is, or what it appears to be. Maybe your friend has worked harder than you know, or she made a smart real-estate investment, or has generous relatives. We rarely see the whole picture. And it could be that your fortunate friend is secretly worried about how she's going to pay *her* mortgage, because that mortgage is bigger than you can imagine, and that means all her bills are commensurately bigger, and the whole nut must be an enormous burden, much more than you could ever dream of.

If one of your friends really does seem to have a successful career, a charmed life, a perfect marriage, a delightful personality, and no money worries, well, that is a rare gift, and you might want to hang around this person and get a few tips.

Don't forget to take stock of what you have accomplished. Instead of looking at your life and thinking that you're not where you're "supposed to be" at this age, make a list of all the many things you have accomplished in the time you've had so far. You may be surprised at how many exciting and interesting activities you've undertaken, and how many natural talents you have. For instance, I can wiggle my ears, and through years of practice can easily move one eyebrow at a time. I can also, in a very disconcerting fashion, cross both my eyes while simultaneously making a circle with my right eye. It's a gift! A gift I will be happy to share with anyone who asks. More often than not, my audience is composed of boys under the age of twelve, who seem to love this trick almost as much as the word "butt" or the sound of farts.

For many years—too many years—I had convinced myself that I was not "successful." I had not attained whatever it was that I had made up in my head that I should have attained by a given age, so therefore, somehow, I was kind of a loser. But at some point, preferably before the age of ninety-five, you really need to have a cold, hard look at what the heck you have been doing for the last forty or fifty years. Have you been learning stuff? Are you interested in learning new stuff? Have you become friends with some good people? Do your friends love you, and do you love them? Do you laugh on a regular basis? Are you excited about what's coming next? Then you're a very, very successful person. Stay engaged, stay interested, and don't forget to celebrate yourself and your successes, great and small, as often as possible!

EXCUSES

"It's too cold; it's too hot; I'm too fat; I don't know anything about that; I'm not good at that sort of thing. I'm really not an athlete; I'm not a very good dancer; I just don't know how; you're the musical one, not me; I can't draw; no one in my family is artistic; I've never been good with numbers; I'm no good at math, just like my mother; I'm just not very handy around the house; I have no idea how people do that; I don't have the time; there isn't enough time. There's never enough time. I'm not pretty enough; I just can't carry a tune; oh, I've never had a green thumb, I can't grow anything; I just know I wouldn't be good at that; I have no rhythm at all; I'm too old to learn a foreign language; I'm too old to learn how to play the piano; I'm too old to learn how to sail; I'll look like an idiot. My family never took me camping, we're not the kind of people who do that; I'm terrible at saving money; I just have no head for business; I'm no good with money; I just don't know where to begin; I don't know the right people; it's all luck anyway, luck and connections; I know I can't do it, so why even try? I'm just not very lucky. I'm too short. I'm too tall. My nose is too big. My teeth are too big. My ears are too big. My feets too big. I just can't get up in front of groups. I'm just a disorganized person. That's just the way I am. No, I don't do that. I used to love that when I was a kid, but I can't do it anymore. I don't have any talent for that; my sister is the artist in the family, not me; my dad could fix anything, I just didn't get the gene; I could have played pro ball, but my parents never signed me up for Little League. I could have traveled around the world, but then I had kids, and I couldn't. Once you have kids, everything changes. That's great for you, but some of us have to work. You're just lucky. You're either born with it or you're not. My hair is too thin. If I were prettier, I would have gotten that job. My life would have been so different if I had never married. My life would have been so different if only I had married. I guess I'm just not meant to be with anyone. Men just can't commit. Women only want a guy with money. Women would like me if I weren't so short. People just don't like me. I'm not good with people. I just wasn't born that way. I just don't have any natural talent. I've always wanted to do that, but it's impossible. Oh, I'm a disaster in the kitchen. I'm hopeless with learning. That's just the way I am, I always have been and I always will be . . ."

Now, speak all your excuses into a large jar with a screw top, or a plastic bag with a twist-tie. Fill that jar or bag up to the top with all those excuses, because you don't need them anymore. Close the top tightly, and take your receptacle outside to the recycling bin.

And yes, I mean you should literally do this. Speak loudly

into the jar or bag. And close it up quickly, and tightly. Dispose of it immediately. Seriously, get that crap out of the house. It might even make you feel better to put all the excuses into a paper or cloth bag, place it in your fireplace, and simply burn it. There. Isn't that better? If it turns out you didn't get rid of all of them in that one sitting, repeat as often as necessary.

I CAN'T DRAW

NEXT TIME YOU WANT TO SAY, "I'M JUST NOT VERY CREATIVE," think about the fact that cooking is a creative pursuit. Putting yourself together in the morning is a creative pursuit. Throwing clothes on is a creative act. If you look at your daily activities as Creative Pursuits, then they won't feel so much like chores. Imagine, say, dusting as a chance to reorganize your precious things, and washing your windows as an opportunity to creatively shine more light on your personal space. Just as garbage collectors got magically transformed into sanitation engineers, you can take the most mundane, everyday tasks and imbue them with a creative spirit. Okay, except cleaning the toilet. That is not the most creative pursuit. But maybe we can hang a few interesting pictures on the wall next to the toilet. Which will make it seem like a more creative space.

Let's say that your daily activities don't involve any cooking, cleaning, or dusting. In fact, you don't know when you last picked up a broom. In fact, how do you even use a broom, again? But you still think you "can't draw." I'm telling you, that is just not the case. If you have no interest in ever, ever drawing any-thing, then that's one thing. But honestly, if you like the idea of it, if you think it would be a really wonderful thing to be able to sit down with a pad and pencil or pen, and create works of art, then I'm telling you, you can do it.

Whoever coined the phrase "It's a poor workman who blames his tools" was a moron. I can just picture his smug little face, doggedly carving a piece of marble with a spoon. I hate that little saying. It's ridiculous and untrue. Yes, Monet probably could have done a fine job with a box of crayons and not complained too much. But see how much better he did with some really nice paints and a fine canvas? I just don't believe that "beginners" should have to endure having their own special brand of lousy tools. Just because you are a novice artist, that doesn't mean you should be forced to create a silk purse out of a sow's ear (which is a darn good little saying, much better than that other one). Of course you think you can't draw, if the last time you tried, some harried teacher shoved a handful of broken Crayolas into your fist and told you to make something fabulous on a sheet of newsprint. Even though crayon on newsprint does have its own charm. But they are two of the more difficult mediums to work with. (I know, sweeping generalization. There are prob-ably scads of artists out there who adore crayons. Then write a book, please, telling us all how to draw with them.)

If you like the idea of making drawings and creating art, then you're much better off if you begin this creative journey with a few good tools. Go to your nearest art supply store. First, just stand in the doorway and feel the excitement. I mean, THE ART SUPPLY STORE!!!!!!!!!! Art supply stores are among the joys of this earth. Enter this mecca of creativity. Saunter slowly up and down each aisle, drinking in the beauty and the possibilities. See what grabs you. Drawing with pencil or pen? Painting with watercolors? Painting with oils or acrylic? All of the above? Paper or canvas? If you think drawing with pencil sounds like fun, you will have a lot of choice when it comes to choosing your pencils. A basic rule of thumb is, if it's marked with a "B" it's soft, if it's marked with an "H" it's hard. "HB" is pretty much right in the middle, and it's a good one to start with. It's your basic Number 2 pencil. So you might want to get a few HB pencils, maybe one 2B and one 2H, so you can play around a little. Get yourself a sharpener, a really good plastic eraser, and a decent sketch pad. If you want to make gifts of your art or do something a little more "finished," try Bristol board, which isn't really board; it's just a very thick paper. The "vellum" surface has a little bit more tooth to it than the "smooth" or "plate" surface.

Pens: Rapidograph 0, 00, or 3X0 are nice thicknesses to try. They make a very fine line. And, of course, my favorite everyday pen for writing and drawing, the very best over-the-counter pen in the world: the Pilot Precise V5 Rolling Ball Extra Fine. Treat yourself to the giant-size box. Because people will steal them. Friends will "accidentally" wander off with your pens. And you'll need the giant box, because you will end up using them for everything. You won't be able to live without this pen.

There are hundreds of colored pencils from which to choose; Prismacolor is actually a brand of colored pencils, even though people often refer to all colored pencils as "Prismacolors," the same way people ask for a "Kleenex" rather than a tissue. I like the regular Prismacolor pencil for some things, because it's a very soft pencil, but I like the fineness of the Prismacolor Verithin, which is good for more detailed work. Same with the Sanford Verithin. I also like the Swiss-made Caran D'ache Supracolor II Soft, But you'll discover your own favorites. Most art supply stores have scratch pads next to the pens and pencils, so artists can try them out.

If you want to do more than play around with your new art supplies, or if you see where you want to go with something but you're not quite sure how to get there, then find a class. Your local university or community college will usually have extension classes offering basic drawing and painting instruction. You might discover a whole new way to express yourself, and a latent talent that's been burning a hole in your pocket.

DOODLE, MORE

Keep scratch pads and pens (like, for instance, I will mention once again the best pen in the world, the Pilot Precise V5 Rolling Ball Extra Fine) by every phone and near where you sit to watch television. That way, when you're talking on the phone, or watching television, you can mindlessly doodle. Because maybe doodling is mindless, but then you end up thinking with a different part of your brain, and seeing with a different part of your eyes, and then all of a sudden you're making art without doing it on purpose. Plus, it's such a good word. Come on, ladies, let's doodle.

DISMOUNT!

My friend Thompy has the best ritual ever, and I would like to take this opportunity to spread the joy. This is a simple exercise that can be done with friends, family, children, or simply as an exercise in solitary exuberance. You know how gymnasts go into those preternatural routines, bending over backward while somehow balancing on a narrow band of wood, then hurling themselves into the air and then landing, with any luck, on their feet, arms lifted in the air?

Well, this little ritual doesn't require years of training, nor does it require waking up at five A.M. every morning for your entire childhood so you can be forced by a gruff Romanian to bend like a pretzel and do flips. In fact, forget the whole "hurling yourself in the air" thing; you could really hurt your back. What you want to do is the dismount part of the whole production: that delightful landing that is taken by those gymnasts upon completion of their routine.

Thompy's Dismount is a lively, congratulatory move that will instantly make you feel at once grounded and celebrated.

Do your dismount when you've completed a task, or heard some good news, or finished the breakfast dishes, or had a heartfelt talk with a friend. Dismount for the hell of it, in celebration of your uniquely exciting and rich life. You don't need to literally jump from a chair. The point is to "stick the landing," in the parlance of underfed twelve-year-old athletes; but this can be done from a standing position. You are going to "land" as if you had just flown down from performing a dizzying display on the balance beam, but the dismount has nothing to do with actual physical prowess. It's all about attitude. It's all about congratulating yourself for a job well done. Congratulate yourself for having a successful day at work, or for making a delicious peanut butter and jelly sandwich. Congratulate yourself for acknowledging the fact that you were tired, and you had a good nap. Congratulate yourself for paying your bills, or sending a thank-you note, or politely telling a telemarketer to put you on the "do not call" list, or for remembering a particularly good joke and managing to tell it properly.

Simply jump up and land solidly, foot forward, arms above your head in a triumphal gesture. Land with a large, beaming smile on your face. You have successfully executed the Dismount. Well done!

IN PRAISE OF MEN

YES, WE LOVE OUR WOMEN FRIENDS. WE ADORE THEM. WE confide in them, they band together and bring us food in times of trouble (thanks, book group!), they are girly and wise and dear. We treasure them, we depend on them; we couldn't live without them. Or at least some of them. A few of them I can kind of do without. In fact, I think some of them are awfully hard on the guys, I really do. I know, I know, what's the deal with me defending men, when, after all, they've been pretty much running the world for a long while and don't exactly need our support.

Well, none of my men friends has been running the world lately, and they're all stand-up, interesting, creative, sensitive, funny, really nice men. My husband included! I think I'm lucky to have such a lot of great guy friends. Some have been friends of mine since before their wives and my husband, some of them are husbands to friends of mine. They are fathers, musicians, writers, filmmakers, accountants, painters, graphic artists, unemployed, gay, straight, bon vivant, shy, gregarious, sports lovers and sports haters, interested and interesting. I value them as I do my close women friends, and I really don't get that whole eye-rolling "Men!" thing in which many women of my acquaintance engage.

My husband, for instance, will often cause a fair amount of eye-rolling when he starts in on a sports rant. He doesn't do it very often, and he'll usually only do it when he finds a fellow enthusiast. This fellow enthusiast may have no idea what he's gotten himself into when he casually says, for example, "Bud Selig had to know what was going on," and suddenly finds himself in a heated discussion on the hypocrisy of Major League Baseball. But what often happens is that certain females in the vicinity will immediately cut loose with the "Not baseball, again!" and the head-shaking, and the "Oh, GOD, guys and sports!" I think this is appalling, and ignorant, and very bad manners. Most of these women are fine when the discourse is centered around their favorite topics and somehow I never hear my husband make loud pronouncements in the middle of a rousing discussion about a recent museum exhibit or television show he's never seen, though he might find the subject matter dull or idiotic. Yet so many women have no compunction against loudly stating their objection should the hint of a sports-related conversation reach their ear. I am not a sports fan; it is not my passion. But I appreciate that my husband is absolutely passionate about it, as perplexing as I might find his interest to be. I love that he's got passions, whether I share all of them or not. He's the kind of guy who knows how to hash out a problem in a thoughtful way, and invariably startles me with his insight. Plus, he makes me laugh, and sometimes writes me songs for my birthday, and you can't beat that with a stick.

My friend Phil loves trailers. If prompted, he will talk at length about any aspect of vintage trailers about which you might have a question. His wife, Lisa, is very understanding. Phil can fix a vintage trailer's plumbing system, install a window, *and* sew curtains. Now, how cool is that? My pal Doug can take clarinets apart *and* put them back together in the proper order, and knows a lot about guitars and saxophones, including how to play them, and is just a pleasant person to sit and talk with. As are my friends Henry and John and Peter, all of whom are capable of making me fall over laughing, each in their own inimitable way. My friend Erik is a fellow fan of hardware stores and gardening centers, and we have been known to tryst at Home Depot for a hot date in the barbecue section. We humor each other's sailing fantasies, and discuss where we're going to build our ocean-view compound, or whether it would be better to sail to the Maldives in a catamaran or a monohull. This is a conversation that my husband would probably prefer to not have with me, so it all works out beautifully.

I really enjoy the company of my men friends, with all their passions and quirks and guy humor. When you talk to guys about stuff, you get a whole different perspective; a perspective that can be just as insightful as that of your most insightful woman friend. I think it's important to have the boys in our lives. I really don't need to "get away" from my husband; we kind of like hanging out together. I don't necessarily want to "escape" for long, bonding holidays with a group of women friends. I mean, sure, that can be a fun thing to do, too. But I don't seek out that kind of escape in order to thrive.

I have two interesting and sensitive sons, and I love that

they've got such a fantastic variety of gents in their lives as role models. Yes, they've got plenty of women too: aunts, best friends, and fairy godmothers who have been cooing over them since they were babies. But there's nothing sweeter than my pal Phil telling me he's going to take my oldest son on a "trip to Tijuana, for some prostitutes and good weed," for his next birthday.

Ha ha! Yes, he's kidding. He's a large, sensitive guy who sews curtains, for crissakes. Give the man a break. Guys are fun, damn it. I'm getting a little over all this precious "my women friends are my strength" stuff. Can't we all sit down together with a bottle of single malt and just hang?

ETIQUETTE AND NICETIES

So I was sitting with a group of friends, having a nice sushi dinner, when somehow the conversation ended up on the topic of a friend's breasts. The topic may have been instigated by the friend in question, or by another friend's husband (we're a friendly bunch), but as this friend's breasts are often remarked upon, being quite remarkable, it wasn't all that unusual. The conversation quickly evolved into a lively back-and-forth between two of my adorably bawdy girlfriends, and then took a turn to vaginas. I realize that taking a turn to vagina-land isn't veering too far off the road if you're already in a heated breast discussion. But the vagina banter? I ask you. Is the vagina banter really necessary? It was unfortunate that our sushi began arriving right in the thick of the vaginal repartee, but there you are. Not to sound overly formal, but O Women of Mystery, must we discuss the vaginas over dinner? If the gents started in with a spirited chat about their penises, discussing at length (sorry!) their respective physiological characteristics loudly and hilariously over appetizers, I wonder if it might have taken the ladies aback. Just a little.

"Hey, Jeff, my cock is so huge! How about yours?" "I just got these great vibrating gloves, man. They rock! I just love to masturbate!" "Whoa, me too, man! But seriously, bare hands is the way to go." And so on.

And so this went on, with lots of delightful details about bodily fluids and the relative merits of various vibrators, with ample (sorry!) breast references thrown in, just because really, the breast talk is hilarious, and I cannot get enough. I adore my friend, and her breasts, but maybe we could talk about politics, or the weather, or any subject to which all of the men and women involved might feel comfortable contributing. Or at least wait until after we've eaten?

If the majority of people in this world now find it completely unobjectionable to discuss the ins and outs (sorry!) of vaginas and penises whilst dining, I feel it is our duty to protect that small minority who are perhaps too shy or uncomfortable discussing their vaginas in a public forum. Perhaps etiquette exists to help us to guard against the tyranny of the majority; or maybe to force us to find different ways to be interesting. You could just let us marvel at your fabulous breasts, secretly. We could all glance down surreptitiously and admire them, and you could be all voluptuous and enigmatic and drink in the admiration, without bringing up the topic at all. Men would swoon, women would sigh, and then later on, after we've all eaten, you and your bestest girlfriends can go off into a corner and discuss the joyful wallop packed by your pocket rockets and vibrating rabbits. Perhaps I'll join you after dessert.

THESE COULD NEVER, ON ANY PLANET
ANYWHERE, EVER BE CONSTRUED AS COMPLIMENTS
(Especially announced in a room full of people.)

(WITH A BIG SMILE.)
"You're such a handsome woman."
"Are you letting your gray grow out? That's so brave of
    you!"
"Has anyone told you that you look like Hillary
    Clinton?"
"You have such a skinny little head!"
"Ooh, when are you due?!"
"Only you could get away with wearing something like
    that."
"I see you've got your 'Aging Hollywood Agent'
    glasses on!"
"I think you look just great as a blonde."
"I love how natural you are, you don't care when your
    eyeliner is smudged."
"You look like that girl in *Heavenly Creatures*, the psycho
    blond one!"
"Your eyes are like marbles."

. . . And I don't know which is worse:
"Wow, you've lost weight!"
or
"Wow, you're so skinny!"

. . . Implying that you were so fat before? Or that now you are so freakishly thin you look unwell? Oh please, please, can we please not continue to compliment our girlfriends on something so banal as how much they weigh? At the very least, it's in rather poor taste to dwell on how "thin" you think someone may be; it could be a sensitive topic, and you might make a friend feel uncomfortable. Surely our friends have many far more interesting attributes about which we might say nice things? Comment instead on their limpid moonlit eyes, or their cheeks that are much like pale fire; compliment the roses in their lips, or the sunny nature of their smile. But you run the risk of sounding like a thoughtless, catty boob when you start in on the "Oh, you've lost so much weight!" Likewise, if someone you haven't seen for a while is expecting a baby, I'm sure she'll let you know when the time seems right. If she doesn't mention it, she is either keeping it a big secret for a good reason, or *she is not pregnant*. It seems obvious, but I urge you to keep your enthusiasm about the impending happy event to yourself, on the very good chance that there is no impending happy event. No gazing at her belly with a knowing smile, no poking at her midsection with loud exclamations, no heartfelt congratulations. Assume that your friend is *not* in the family way, and if you can manage to keep yourself from making any other boneheaded comments, you may still have a friend when the encounter has run its course.

ACCENTUATE YOUR POSITIVES!

I SO MUCH APPRECIATE, AT LEAST IN THEORY, THE ZEN-LIKE, uncluttered, ecru-on-ecru living spaces pictured in the far too many home decor magazines to which I subscribe. And yet I often find myself asking, "Um, where's all their stuff?" How is it they have no stacks of books piled on the coffee table, alongside a game of fifty-two pickup and some scattered sheet music? Are these people ashamed of their relatives? Where are the photos of Mom and Dad, and the baby pictures? Have they actually paid a visit to their own living rooms? Do they honestly cook in that kitchen? And then I come to the dawning realization that yes, they probably have, and they probably do (or at least their private chef does), they just happen to be neater, wealthier, more organized, and probably smarter and more interesting than I am. And then all I can see are the giant cracks above the back door of my house, where the foundation is sinking, and the way the light switch in the bathroom kind of hangs off the wall, and the fact that the legs on the crappy orange sofa are literally about to break for real this time and everyone will probably come crashing to the floor next time they sit down to watch TV.

Snap out of it! Before we spiral down into a pit of despair, let's take a cold, hard look at what we do have. Our health? Two good legs and a mouth that works, nonstop if need be? A roof over our heads, no matter how many holes it may have? Can we find some good among the crap? And can we take the good that we do have, and make more of it? Well, let's just say you have a few walls holding up that roof over your head. Perhaps a nice coat of colorful paint might perk things up.

I have often been told that I am "so brave" because I have painted the walls of my house with very bright colors. But I would like to set the record straight. Running into a burning house to rescue a child is brave. Standing up against a totalitarian government when faced with prison or torture, that is brave. Insulting a large, angry person who is carrying a pointy stick, that is brave. Or stupid. Or both. Jumping on a runaway train so you can stop it before it flies off the bridge that Lex Luthor blew up, that's really brave. Painting your house in bold, bright colors is not brave.

It's paint. It can be painted over in less time than it will take you to grow out a bad haircut. So my advice is, don't paint your walls white unless you really love love love the absence of color. Don't paint your walls beige because you're worried about the "resale value," unless you're planning on putting your house on the market next week. Surround yourselves with the colors that make you happy. Surround yourselves with pictures that make you happy.

You can put a frame on just about anything, and it will look like ART. If you don't have any art on your walls, and have always wanted some, find a child to make you some art. If you don't have any children of your own, ask a friend's child. You might think, "I don't want a bunch of kiddie art on my walls, that will look tacky." But I'm telling you, put a frame around it, and voilà! Your very own piece of Outsider art. Go to the thrift store and find some old LPs, frame four of them, and arrange them as a set. It doesn't even matter if they're the coolest album covers in the world; they will all be uniform in size, and will somehow all look very cool together. You can match them by complimentary colors, and you can match them by subject matter or type of music.

And all that excess junk you may have lying around? Turn that random junk into a *Collection*. As in, "My Collection of beer caps is prominently displayed next to my Collection of early twenty-first-century wine corks." Here's how to make your junk into a collection: categorize your junk by shape, common color, era, or other similarity. Then simply arrange artful groups of your junk on a shelf, or in a display case. Even if your various individual pieces of junk have nothing in common with one another, group it together in some way. Because artful groupings of junk make it look as if you have a keen eye for junk, and have actually been collecting junk on purpose. You are a junk connoisseur. You know your junk.

But what about the hanging light switch and the cracks in the wall? Let's say you mean to eventually remodel your bathroom. You know what you'd like to do, but you aren't currently able to do any of it, due to the fact that you don't happen to have an extra twenty thousand dollars lying around so that you can make your bathroom more pleasant. Other than the plumbing, which, thankfully, works as it's supposed to, at least most of the time, your bathroom is kind of a wreck. The paint is chipping; there are enormous, geologic fault-size cracks running the length of the wall, the floor is some kind of hideous ocher vinyl installed in 1979, and the whole thing is just, well, butt-ugly. It is not a happy bathroom. You do your business and you want to get out of there. Well, one way to perk up this small interior-design blight is to just make a large, tasty load of lemonade with those nice, juicy lemons.

In the case of my hideous bathroom, there just wasn't much I could do that would fit my modest budget, which is usually about fifteen dollars. So I assessed some of the junk I had lying around (see "collection") and realized that I had a certain amount of vaguely Hawaiian-themed objects and ephemera. An old piece of sheet music that my friends Peter and Rosina had given me ("Oh How She Could Yakki Hakki Wikki Wakki Woo"), a couple of greeting cards my friend Gail had sent from Maui, an old postcard of a hula girl that I had enlarged on a color copy machine, some plastic tropical fish I found in a toy box, a remnant of Hawaiian-print fabric, and two framed prints of palm trees. Okay, fine, I have a hard time throwing things away.

In any event, since the horrible shower tiles were trimmed in a dull sky-blue, I painted the shower ceiling in a vivid turquoise, which made the other blue bits more bearable. I found an old frame for the sheet music, and bought a few inexpensive frames for the postcards and the hula girl picture. I glued some squares of gold leaf onto the walls (just because I found some gold-leaf squares in a drawer) and nailed the tropical plastic fishes to the wall next to the medicine cabinet. Just like they're swimming! Very festive. The fabric remnant became a curtain for the window, using curtain clips purchased from the hardware store (no sewing!) and a bamboo pole curtain rod cut from the front yard. The curtain is a bright Hawaiian pattern, and masterfully manages to mask the cracked window. I found a book about old Hawaii, scanned and copied some of my favorite surfer and hula girl images, and used decoupage glue to affix the images to the doors of the sink cabinet. I may just go crazy and decoupage the whole bathroom with hula girls, because it looks a lot happier than what it looked like before I gave it an attack of Hawaiiana. Now it's a happy, harmonious hula hideaway, with a toilet.

The really good thing about having a dilapidated bathroom is that it really frees you up to go to town with the paint and the fun. Chances are, when my bathroom finally gets gutted and redone, and I get my pretty stone floor and mosaic-tile walls, and polished teak sink cabinet and built-in shelves and gleaming window that actually opens, I might be less apt to slap a picture of a naked hula girl on the wall. And that would be a shame.

(So maybe I'll do it anyway.)

Paint your fireplace mantel HOT PINK.

Paint your front door CANARY YELLOW.

Paint your dining room TANGERINE.

HOME DECORATING: FENG SHUI
(NO, IT'S NOT PRONOUNCED FENG SHUI)

If a friend gives you a book on feng shui (fung shway!), accept it gratefully. It may be your friend's very gentle way of telling you that you have too much stuff. Someone will, eventually, give you one of those handy tomes, so there is really no need to go out and purchase a stack of them, thereby collecting more stuff, which you will then need to find a place to put.

The essence of feng shui is simple and sensible: throw out a bunch of stuff, clear out your clutter, put a vase of flowers somewhere, and oh, make sure you face the door when sitting at your desk. The Mafia handbook will tell you much the same thing, by the way. Open a window. There, now, isn't that better?

It's essentially good advice, so of course it had to become a New Age industry. Armies of feng shui practitioners are now available to clear not only our chi but our wallets. To the tune of hundreds of dollars. For a consultation. That's not counting the cost of all the lucky bamboo, crystal balls, and prosperity coins, which will provide you with yet more clutter.

There is really no need to hang lots of mirrors in disconcerting places. Your guests may not care to be confronted with their windblown visages upon entering your house, preferring to freshen up in the privacy of the loo. Likewise, you need not put furniture at odd angles because a book told you it would be fortuitous. Honestly, are your tenuous fortunes really going to suddenly turn around because you rearranged your sofa at a very inconvenient angle? Is it worth the ensuing lawsuits when your guests trip over it every time they enter your living room? And do you really need that fountain inside, over in the corner? Doesn't the sound of it just make you want to pee?

And what's with all the mirrors? Aren't you just inviting years of bad luck if one of them should break?

There are many people who wholeheartedly endorse the practice of feng shui, to the point of buying or not buying a house (a whole house!) or condo based on a feng shui practitioner telling them whether the rooms are facing the right way. That is their prerogative. Of course they should make an enormous life decision based solely on whether the front door faces east or south. It's an ancient Chinese practice that will bring you luck! Just like it did the billions of Chinese living under a brutal totalitarian regime. So really, put a giant and expensive fish in that giant fish tank that now sits proudly in your front hall. And just because everyone on the West Side has painted their door red, it doesn't mean it's too trendy. Really! It's Good Luck!

Resist the temptation to fork over your next month's mortgage to a highly paid fortune-teller, and do a big spring cleaning instead.

Save your money with these simple tips:

- Get rid of your TV. That's right. You will open up your paths of chi and gain newfound wealth, by losing that costly cable bill.

- While you sit at your newly uncluttered desk, tilt your head toward the northwest. It's fortuitous. And free!

- Pick up some of that junk that's starting to propagate in the corner. It's easy and refreshing. Walk around the room with a couple of paper bags, one for recycling and one for garbage.

- Move your furniture around from time to time, and change the pictures on the walls. It's the least expensive and easiest way to redecorate.

- Unless you are a practicing Buddhist—that shrine in the corner of your dining room? Honestly, it's starting to look like a dim sum restaurant in there.

SHRINE ON

Sometimes I say things and then afterward I think about what I said, and I think, "Really? Do I really think that? Wasn't that kind of a nasty thing to say, about having a shrine in your house?" Well, you're right, it was very unkind. Because having a little shrine in your house can be a lovely thing, and a fun way to honor something meaningful in your life. It can be a shrine to your great vacation, a shrine to celebrate your friends or family, a shrine to your joyful self. A shrine to remind you to celebrate, a shrine to commemorate all the beautiful things in your life that you've done, or a shrine to all of the exciting and adventurous things you intend to do: a shrine to all the great dresses you've ever had, a shrine to romance, a shrine to your creative soul.

Your shrine can be as simple or elaborate as you want to make it. Create a shrine on a dedicated shelf or small table, or create a little grouping of meaningful objects on the corner of a bookshelf. Or you could craft a freestanding shrine or a wall-mounted shrine from an old wooden wine crate or cigar box. Line the back with a piece of cork cut to fit—and you've got a surface on which to pin a variety of pictures, found or familiar objects, fortune-cookie fortunes, Mardi Gras beads, or your grandfather's watch. Then, on the inside shelf part of the box, you can place a small pillar candle or tea light, surrounded by more objects that have special meanings for you. A small bud vase to hold a fresh flower could be placed there too, because fresh flowers are always nice to have in a shrine.

A shrine is not only a way to honor something meaningful, it can be a great way to exhibit a bunch of junk you have lying around that you have no idea what to do with. You can make a Shrine to Childhood! In it will go the head from that beautiful doll your sisters gave you for Christmas, the body of which was chewed up by the dog; in it will go some special childhood photographs, a favorite childhood book, a tiny sofa from your dollhouse. Or how about a shrine to Love, or Old Boyfriends? I have an actual clay cast of an ex-boyfriend's baby finger, for instance. Now, what in the world am I going to do with that? Well, well,

well, what a perfect object for a shrine! I will line a box with old love letters and Valentines, and display whatever other objects might be appropriately reminiscent of that time in my life. A candle, that miniature cast-metal duck holding a machine gun (a romantic gift), a few old photographs, and there you have not only a shrine but a piece of art. And a sure icebreaker next time you have a few friends over, as they'll be certain to ask you the provenance of each item. Your shrine can be a visual commemoration of your life so far, or simply a reminder to celebrate it. And if you're about to reach a certain milestone birthday that you'd like to memorialize, a lovely little homemade shrine is a lot less permanent than a tattoo.

REUSE, RECYCLE, AND REARRANGE

WHEN TIMES ARE A LITTLE TIGHT, AS THEY CAN OFTEN BE, one of the most affordable and easiest ways to make your dwelling fresh and new is to simply rearrange the furniture. You can switch furniture from one room to another, or rearrange it within the same room. You can rearrange the pictures on the walls, or group them a different way. For instance, I noticed I had a few black-and-white pictures hanging on various walls—a few paintings, several black-and-white photographs, a few black-and-white prints, a few black-and-white line drawings. I gathered up these black-and-white pieces and hung them all on the same wall, together. It looked absolutely stunning, as if I had been specifically collecting interesting black-and-white art for years.

Much to my husband's chagrin, I still find it difficult to resist bringing home furniture that I have found on the street. I'm not talking about sofas or mattresses, because you don't really know what might be living in something upholstered; but I have found a few lovely chairs that only needed a little polishing or some new upholstery; a gorgeous mid-century teak side-table that just needed a little polishing and a small bit of glue; and, once, a flat slab of marble that only had one chipped corner.

Scavenging for furniture may not, understandably, be your cup of tea, but for less than it costs to buy new furniture, you can reupholster your existing furniture, which is as much fun as buying a new dress. Let's say you have a big armchair. It's really comfortable, but kind of ugly or drab. Well, take yourself down to the fabric shop, and go to town. If you have a living room full of country-French floral, perhaps now is the time to trade in for a mod orange vinyl, or a regal gold brocade. You might find some stunning fabric that's a little too shockingly bright, or maybe just too pricey for an entire sofa or your large overstuffed lounger, but a small amount of it could be used to redo the cushion on that formerly dull little chair that's always sat unnoticed in the corner, and, well, it will no longer sit unnoticed in the corner. Start exploring unexpected and interesting color combinations. Cover your off-white sofa in a dark lime-green slipcover, with lemon-yellow throw pillows, or reupholster it in orange linen, with hot-pink accent pillows, or aquamarine blue with brown accents; or do everything in a bright mustard yellow. And if you really do have a living room full of country-French floral, it is definitely time for a little change.

CLEAN YOUR ROOM!! THE HOME OFFICE

Sometimes you really don't need a whole new home-office suite. Sometimes you don't need to spend three thousand dollars on a new shelving system. Sometimes you just need to clean your room. You will be amazed, surprised, perhaps even shocked at the transformation that occurs when you give a room a good, solid cleaning. And it is even kind of fun, if you decide ahead of time that you can devote an entire day (or two) to the enterprise.

First sweep the room with your eyes. Take in each corner. Try to see it with new eyes. Perhaps you'll start noticing your unintended still-life arrangements, the detritus of your every-day life that has accumulated into small tableaux, like modern Dutch masters; but instead of bowls of grapes and a dead pheasant, you have little piles of catalogs, books, articles you've cut out, a half-full cup of coffee and a banana peel, old bills, your collection of turquoise California pottery jammed up against a stack of books. Piles of things seem to have taken up permanent residence, piles of stuff you have simply stopped noticing. You need to take notice. You need to put all this stuff into a big box, and then sort out the bills from the important documents from the nine catalogs left over from last spring.

You'll need some garbage bags or paper grocery bags; a few for recycling, a few for garbage, and a few for those things you're not sure you want to throw away. Because you're going to go around the room and clear it out completely, even your books and your candles and the stuff you want to keep. You don't have to decide exactly what you're going to throw away right now, this minute, if the thought makes you nervous. But you need to get everything off every surface so you can see the bones of the room again. You may end up taking those things you're not sure you want to throw away, and arranging them differently, in another room, or you may decide to rotate some of them; you may decide that your three vintage radios don't necessarily have to be displayed along with all of your poetry books, your collection of hatboxes, and your coconut monkey. I love that weird incense burner that your boyfriend gave you in college, and I, too, just adore the way those stacks of magazines are lined up in neat little piles against the wall of the room, and the way you've artfully mounded your catalogs, bills, to-do notes, pens, and old cell phones next to your computer, along with all those wires; it looks so nonchalant and carefree, really. But when you simply remove the entire roomful of clutter, including the furniture that's not too heavy to move yourself, you'll discover a whole new room, a blank canvas, a new void that may be swept clean, dusted, polished, then slowly and conscientiously filled.

So clear the whole thing, as best as you can. Then walk around the room, and imagine it arranged in a number of different ways. Put your favorite chair in there; imagine where you'd like your desk to be. If you are putting a home office in a corner of another all-purpose room, imagine how you can make the best use of your existing furniture. Maybe that low bookshelf can be placed alongside your desk to make an L-shaped desk configuration. But the important thing is, clean your room from time to time; and not just the sweeping, dusting, and vacuuming kind of cleaning. Upend your room, clear out the corners, and you have a brand-new room, for a lot less trouble and expense than moving to a whole new house.

PART V

IN CASE THE FLYING TURTLES THAT PROTECT
THE EARTH GET HIT BY ALIEN GAMMA RAYS

SURVIVAL SKILLS FOR
THE MATURE WOMAN

PERHAPS THERE ARE CERTAIN AREAS OF YOUR KNOW-HOW
that have been inadvertently neglected. For instance, you may
have never learned how to tie a good knot, or how to change a
tire. But at this point in your life, you've got AAA for your flat tires
and perhaps a devoted sailor friend who can make knots for you
on demand. You're thinking: "I've made it this far without having
to employ a buntline hitch, what the hell. Let's live dangerously."

Well, your life may not depend on having certain life-skills,
but what if it did? What if no one was able to roast marshmallows because *you couldn't build a fire*? What if all the grocery
stores ran out of baby lettuce, and you had no idea how to grow
any? Imagine, if you will, running out of your favorite facial
mask, and Barneys has *closed*, due to renovation or apocalypse.
Or this possible nightmare scenario: you wake up one morning
and realize that you just spent $185 on a scrub and a toner and
there is no money left for dinner, for the next several nights.
It suddenly dawns on you that you could have made your own
scrub and toner from ingredients sitting in your own cupboards
and refrigerator, *if only you knew how!*

It's never too late to learn a few simple survival skills, tricks that may not only help you in the Great Outdoors—on the off chance you ever decide to venture out there—they can help you have a lovely life in the comfort of your own home. At the very least, you will impress your friends with your heretofore-unknown array of survivalist talents. The more practical knowledge you have the more interesting and well-rounded you will be. Practical knowledge not only makes you a more complex and fascinating person, it is, well, practical. It's a secret source of pride to know that—even though I am a city girl—I know how to build a campfire. I also know how to gut and clean a fish, make fabric dye out of onion skins, make a s'more, and grow vegetables in a small square-foot garden. Also, may I tell you more? Because I kind of never pat myself on the back enough about this stuff. But I know how to harvest worm castings and order ice cream in French. Sure, I have friends who can pretty much order anything they want in French because they speak it fluently, but with survival skills, it's the breadth of completely random knowledge that counts. Many people may speak French fluently, but can they also sing at least fifty songs that were written before 1935 *and* make great deviled eggs? It is doubtful. I also know many tasty things to do with kale. Give me a piece of raw salmon, and I can make gravlax from scratch (see page 219). If you gave me a handful of freshly shorn sheep's wool, I could make yarn out of it. Also, I know that if suddenly told we had to live with no electricity or gas and/or takeout food, I could whip together some delicious meals from my store of canned goods in the pantry; I could forage for food in the backyard, make my own facial scrubs and moisturizer, and build a fire. And we all can! Because, let's just say the economy should take a little dive, for instance. Let's just *say*. Wouldn't you rather be one of those fabulous women who knows how to make her own beer in the cellar and cook dandelion greens than the kind who falls apart when a nail chips or Whole Foods discontinues her favorite energy bar?

Having a decent range of survival skills doesn't require you to start stocking ammo and living out of a bunker. But wouldn't it be nice to know that you could get by in a pinch? Wouldn't it be a good feeling to be able to pass on to sons, daughters, and younger friends certain nuggets of wisdom that were passed down to you? And if you have never been camping in your life, or if your grandmother never showed you how to make pickles, well, it's never too late to bolster that bit of a gap in your life-skills education. "But I hate to camp," you might be saying right now, as you look up from Anthony Lane's latest review and sip your freshly pressed Guatemalan Antigua. "This review is hilarious, and reading *The New Yorker* while sipping coffee is much better than camping. You are a crazy lady who keeps ducks in the backyard. Get out of my apartment." Okay, fine. But you know, a fabulous woman can know how to use a French press *and* how to clean a floor with vinegar, which works incredibly well, I might add. Just don't use the good balsamic.

> *Je voudrais la café crème glacée,*
> *s'il vous plaît. Il semble trés bon. Merci!*

> *(I would like the coffee ice cream, please.*
> *It looks very good. Thank you!)*

HOW TO BUILD A GOOD FIRE

You may already be a champion fire builder, but if it's something you just never got around to learning, well, what better time than now? Maybe you have never been camping, or you live in an apartment with no fireplace; you have never had an opportunity to build a fire, nor do you foresee having to build a fire anytime in your future. Fair enough. But it's still a good skill to possess. Especially for us city dwellers; you want to have skills like this that you can pull out of your back pocket and surprise people with. You want to be able to step in and offer genuine assistance, should you be at a party and see your panicked host or hostess struggling with a pile of balled-up newspapers in front of their fireplace. Or maybe you'll be in a cabin in the woods someday, it could happen! Or someone will take you on your first camping trip. Or civilization, as we know it, will end. There are so many, many reasons you should know how to build a fire.

Whether in a campfire ring or a home fireplace, the essentials are the same. But let's start with the campfire, because it just sounds more survivalist, and, practically speaking, it's a skill you might need should you find yourself in the woods, in the dark, feeling damp and chilled. You should make your fire in a fire ring; if you don't have one, dig a shallow pit and ring it with large rocks. If there's one handy, butt your fire ring up against a large boulder; it will act as sort of a chimney.

You'll need tinder, which would be any kind of small, dried twigs or moss—anything light and flammable. Balled-up newspaper works too, as will the paper plates off of which you ate dinner. Anything that will help ignite the kindling. You'll need kindling—bigger twigs, sticks, and branches. Anything that will catch fire and will stay lit long enough to ignite a larger log. Then you'll need some medium and large logs. You'll want to gather all of your materials before you start your fire. If you have children, send them to find and fetch twigs, branches, and logs, as their eyes are probably better than yours. You can take this opportunity to pour yourself a little something to take the chill off while you put the finishing touches on your fire ring.

Build your fire from the bottom up. Make a little pile of tinder (you can put your balled-up newspaper in this pile). Just leave some air spaces, so the fire can breathe. Next, construct a teepee of the kindling: the slightly larger branches and sticks. Then place some larger pieces of wood in sort of a log-cabin structure around your teepee. Stick a long match into the inner pile of kindling, and watch it go. When it looks as if the bigger pieces of wood have really caught, you may lay one or two large pieces across the top as needed. If it starts getting smoky, just poke at it a little with a stick, to give it some oxygen.

Dried citrus peels are an excellent fire-starter; next time you eat an orange, tangerine, or clementine, save the peel. Place the citrus peels in a mesh colander or lay them out on some newspaper. Something well-ventilated, so they'll dry out without growing mold. When the peels are all dried out, start collecting them in a container, and keep this container by your fireplace. Or, if you have no fireplace, keep the peels handy for the next time you take a camping trip. The oils in the dried citrus peels cause them to ignite, in case you're low on tinder, or just need a little extra help starting your fire. Keep long sticks handy for marshmallow roasting, indoors and out. And a bucket of water nearby, just in case. Also, guitars are nice to have around, and friends who play them well, so you can all start singing once the fire really gets going.

HOW TO MAKE A S'MORE

Of course you've had a s'more, but maybe you haven't had one for a very long time, or the part of the brain that used to remember how to make them got all filled up with passwords and the names of *American Idol* winners. Anyhoo, you'll need:

Graham crackers
Dark chocolate squares
Marshmallows

Roast your marshmallow on a stick. Some people prefer the "scorch and burn" method, but I think the best s'mores involve a golden-toasty-brown marshmallow with a hot, gooey center. Place your chocolate square on your graham cracker square, and your hot marshmallow on top of the chocolate. Top with another graham cracker square to sandwich the marshmallow-chocolate combo. Eat while hot. And then make s'more!

EVERY GAL SHOULD KNOW AT LEAST ONE GOOD CAMPFIRE SONG

You Are My Sunshine

The other night, dear, as I lay sleeping
I dreamed I held you in my arms.
When I awoke, dear, I was mistaken
So I lay my head down and I cried.

(chorus)
You are my sunshine, my only sunshine.
You make me happy when skies are gray.
You'll never know, dear, how much I love you.
Please don't take my sunshine away.

I'll always love you and make you happy
If you will only say the same.
But if you leave me and love another
You'll regret it all someday.

(Chorus)
You told me once, dear, you really loved me
And no one else could come between.
But now you've left me and love another.
You have shattered all of my dreams.

(chorus)
In all my dreams, dear, you seem to leave me.
When I awake, my poor heart pains.
So when you come back and make me happy,
I'll forgive you, dear, I'll take all the blame.
(chorus)
You are my sunshine, my only sunshine.
You make me happy when skies are gray.
You'll never know, dear, how much I love you.
Please don't take my sunshine away.

IN CASE THE GIANT SPIDERS COME AND WE CAN'T GET TO SEPHORA

THE PANTRY—YOUR HOME BEAUTY SUPPLY STORE

[*] Mix Quaker Oats with a little olive oil for a mild gommage; gently rub on face, neck, and body. (Do not use the McCann's steel-cut oats, because ow that could hurt!) Or make a scrub with 2 tsp oatmeal, 2 tsp dried milk, and 1 tsp ground cinnamon. Add just enough water to make a paste. Apply to face gently, in small, circular motions. You can mix some baking soda with a handful of oatmeal, add enough water to make a paste, and use it as an exfoliating scrub. Yum!

[*] Salt or sugar mixed with a little olive or coconut oil makes an excellent facial scrub. In fact, you can use it on your entire body, and you will feel silky-smooth afterward. You might want to stand in the bathtub while you apply it. Add ground coffee to the sugar and olive oil paste, for a caffeinated cellulite scrub. You might want to put something over the drain when you do this one, as the coffee grounds don't dissolve quite the way the sugar and salt do.

[*] I keep a jar of coconut oil in my kitchen, because it's better than olive oil for cooking with high heat. Plus, it's nice for facial massages, and you can dab it on your lips if they feel dry while you're sautéing up some zucchini.

[*] Honey, honey, honey: it's a natural humectant, an antioxidant, and apparently is such a good antibacterial it can be used as a treatment for wounds infected with antibiotic-resistant bacteria. We should be covering ourselves in this stuff, morning, noon, and night. But for a start: tie your hair back and dab it on your face (not too thick, because it'll drip), then gently tap your fingers on your face. Tap your fingers up and down and all around your face; the honey will start getting tacky. This is a soothing but mindless exercise best undertaken while watching either TV or paint drying. Rinse with warm water after 15 or 20 minutes. You can also mix some honey with a little organic milk. Stir it up and apply, rinsing after 15 minutes.

Raw honey is best, and it'll keep for a few years in a cool, dark place. Don't forget to mix it with a little lemon and eat it when you have a sore throat or laryngitis. It's not just soothing and tasty, you know; the antibacterial properties will really help you get better.

[*] We must all bow down and worship the mighty olive, for giving us such beautiful oil into which we can dip our bread for eating, and our fingers for making our skin beautiful. Use it in your hair, gently massage your face with it, use it on chapped

lips, dab it under your eyes, moisturize your hands and feet
with it, put a few drops in your bathwater, in fact just bathe in
it. It's that good. Olive oil! For your inside and out.

[*] Soak a cotton ball with milk, rub it on your face, and
let it dry. Buttermilk works well, too. And plain yogurt, if
you have any. Now, what if we mixed the buttermilk or plain
yogurt in with, say, some honey? Oatmeal? The mind reels.
Try it!

[*] Avocado!! Another ingenious idea from the same Magic
Edible Food Fairy that brought you honey; not only delicious to
eat but good for you, and an excellent moisturizing mask. Next
time you open up an avocado, just mash up a sliver of it and
spread it on your face, especially on those days you just don't
have the time to mix up some crazy honey-buttermilk-oatmeal
concoction. Leave on for 15 minutes. Try to get it rinsed off
before your sister and her new boyfriend, who you had no
idea were flying in from Vancouver to surprise you for your
birthday, arrive at the back door with cake.

[*] Mash a banana and spread it on your face and neck.

[*] If you've peeled an orange or tangerine and are about to
eat it, take a piece of it and rub the juice all over your face. Let it
dry, then rinse. You can use two halves of a grape as a cleanser.
I guess it's like a fruit-acid peel, but with real fruit instead of
chemicals. Whoa. What a concept. If you are at a sushi bar and
they give you a plate of really nice sectioned oranges, do not

take one and rub it all over your face, for heaven's sake, there's a time and a place for that sort of thing.

[*] Blend a few chunks of pineapple with some olive oil, and use it as a mask for your face.

[*] Mash ½ cup overripe strawberries (the ones you were going to throw out anyway), with the tops cut off, with ¼ cup of cornstarch. Apply to your face and leave on for 15 minutes. Just before rinsing, scrub it into your face in a circular motion. Waste not, want not!

[*] Grate or blend a cold cucumber. Apply to your face, eyes, neck, lips, all over. Lie down (on a towel, expect drips) in a comfortable position, perhaps with some music playing. When I go to the Korean spa, the cold grated cucumber that the nice Korean women slather on my face after a bracing scrub is sheer HEAVEN.

GROW YOUR OWN SALAD

IT'S REALLY NOT THAT DIFFICULT, AND EVEN IF YOU LIVE IN an apartment with no backyard, you can easily have a pot with baby lettuces or herbs sitting on your balcony or back porch. And if you have a small plot of garden, even only a few square feet, you've got enough space for salad, herbs, and tomatoes.

So: Go to a nursery, or go online; buy yourself a packet of mixed mesclun, or "salad mix," or purchase a few seedlings of basil, parsley, dill, oregano, tarragon; preferably herbs you like to use for cooking, tea, or health and beauty remedies. If you don't have a compost pile, you might want to purchase a small bag of amendment, and maybe even a bag of potting soil if your soil looks like hard-packed barren wasteland. Of course if you're doing it all in a big container, you'll need enough potting soil to fill it nearly to the top. Follow the directions on the seed packet, but you needn't pour the seeds on; you'll only be thinning them as they shoot up. Why not save some seeds, and yourself the trouble of thinning the herd, by planting fewer seeds in the first place? Your lettuces and herbs will want some sun, but not blazing sun all day long, or everything will bolt too quickly. Tomatoes will need full sun, and a lot of it; so plan your garden accordingly.

Go to the bookstore and library; use Google as a gardening resource. Ask friends who know a little bit about gardening to give you some tips. In a very short time, you should be able to bring a basket outside in the early evenings to harvest a little salad for dinner. In the fall and winter, replace your lettuce garden with chard, kale, and other greens. Even a small herb garden on your windowsill can be a happy and satisfying experience. Yes, I know you can buy parsley, but anyone can *buy* parsley. How about being able to snip a little off your windowsill plant to throw over a salad, or a few stalks of your own dill in a lovely fall potato soup? Those cucumbers growing up the side of your wall can be put into salads, and cucumber chunks can be added to a pitcher of cold water along with a handful of lemon slices for the most refreshing thirst-quencher. And let's not forget how you can shred them over your face and place slices over your baggy eyes.

Before long you will be ripping out the lawn on your local traffic median, or sneaking over to the neighbor's backyard to put in your spring plantings. I'm not an expert, but Google "urban farming," "urban gardening," "edible landscapes," or simply "planting herbs and lettuces" in your particular neck of the planet. You'll find more resources than you'll know what to do with, certainly enough to get you started. Start a compost pile! It has become a very chic thing to do; and if it hasn't yet become all the rage where you live, be the first on your block to keep a worm bin under your sink. All the girls will want one, and it will become the must-have accessory for the season. It's a guaranteed conversation starter (can you say "vermiculture?"), and the resultant worm castings will magically fertilize those herbs you're now growing in that sunny kitchen window. Ain't life grand?

MAKE YOUR OWN HOMEMADE SWEDISH GRAVLAX FROM A SLAB OF RAW SALMON

This is one of the most deceptively simple dishes you will ever make. I can't believe I am even telling you this. It's kind of a specialty of mine for the holidays, but it's delicious and easy enough to make any time of year, especially those months when inexpensive wild salmon is readily available. I learned this recipe from my Swedish sister-in-law Ginger, who was a genius in the kitchen and could whip up a smorgasbord without batting an eyelash. You will need to make your gravlax at least two days ahead of time (so plan ahead), and you will need a brick or a six-pack of sodas, to use as a weight. But honestly, when you bring this out for dinner, people will not believe you made it yourself. It's the kind of thing that people *buy,* they don't *make* it. It's like bringing out a side of salted beef from a hook in the basement and telling everyone you've been making your own corned beef. And with a side dish of cold dilled potatoes and some pickled cucumbers, you've got a festive, easy meal that can be made in advance.

For your *gravad lax,* you will need:

A middle cut of fresh wild salmon
¼ cup coarse salt
¼ cup sugar

1 tbsp peppercorns, crushed

2 large bunches fresh dill

¼ cup of gin

Lemon wedges

DRESSING

3 tbsp extra-virgin olive oil

2 tsp vinegar

1 ½ tsp Dijon mustard

¼ tsp salt

Dash of pepper

Dash of sugar

Clean, rinse, and dry the salmon. Cut the fish along the back, removing the bone, or ask your nice fishmonger to cut the fish for you, leaving you two equal-size center cuts of salmon that fit together. Sometimes, when I'm making a small amount of gravlax for dinner, I just get two pieces of salmon that are already cut, making sure they are fairly uniform in size and will fit together nicely.

Mix the salt, sugar, and crushed peppercorns in a bowl, and place a thick layer of dill sprigs on the bottom of a shallow baking pan or dish. Rub both pieces of salmon with gin and set on a plate. Rub part of the dry salt/sugar mixture into the fish, and lay one piece skin-side down on top of the dill. Sprinkle with more dry seasonings and top with plenty of dill sprigs. Set other piece of salmon, skin-side up, on top of the salmon in the pan; sprinkle with remaining dry mixture and cover with dill sprigs. Cover loosely with plastic wrap and set a board on top of the fish. Weigh down the fish with a brick or a six-pack of soda. Refrigerate at least 24 hours, but preferably 2 to 4 days.

Remove from the pan, scrape the spices off the salmon, and place on a cutting board. Cut the salmon into medium slices, arrange on a serving platter, and garnish with fresh dill and lemon wedges. Whisk together the ingredients for the dressing, and serve with the salmon. Depending on how large your middle cut of salmon is, this should make from 6 to 10 servings.

NATURAL DYES FROM HOUSEHOLD STUFF

Onion skins can be saved and used to dye your boring white cotton, silk, or wool garments a lovely shade of golden brown. Beets, as you know if you've ever made a salad with them, will dye anything a dark magenta-red. If you mix the two, you'll get sort of an orange-y color. Black tea bags and coffee grounds will impart a pale brown antiqued look to anything white or pastel. I learned this at camp, along with carding, spinning, and weaving. Thanks, Tam and Clive!

Boil the onion skins or cut-up beets in a large stockpot with ½ cup of salt per 8 cups of water, or one part white vinegar per four parts water. Boil for a few hours and strain. Add your white cotton, silk, or wool clothing, yarn, or tie dye–ready T-shirts and let simmer for an hour or more. For a more intense color, turn the heat off after an hour or so and let sit overnight. Washed fabric tends to hold the color better.

Experiment with pomegranate (the rind apparently makes a nice yellow dye) and frozen grape juice, a few cans of which make a lovely lavender color, like a refreshing sherbet.

YOUR ALTOID TIN BOX SURVIVAL KIT

INGREDIENTS

Ten strike-anywhere matches, held with a rubber band.

Band-Aids and 2 butterfly closures

2 small packets antibiotic ointment

2 needles, wrapped with black thread

A plastic garbage bag, rolled to fit and tied with a rubber
band

Reynolds Oven Bag (for a water bag)

20 Potable Aqua water purification tablets

20mm AA liquid-filled button compass

Commando Wire Saw (small survival cable saw)

2 feet of aluminum foil for making a cup, signaling,
cooking fish

Small emergency candle, cut to fit

Baggie filled with petroleum jelly–soaked cotton balls to
use as tinder. (They light with one spark!) (Okay, it
might be a little bit of a stretch to get a whole baggie
filled with cotton balls into an Altoid box. But three or
four will definitely fit.)

Keep this handy tin (okay, maybe you'll need two) in the
glove-box of your car, or in the pocket of your coat when you
go on long car trips. In case you take the scenic route, and the
Toxic Swamp Monsters finally come, or you find yourself in
the middle of a dark mountain pass with a flat tire and no cell
phone reception, and there's a flash flood and electrical storm
and you are miles from civilization. Always carry extra water

in your car, for this very reason, and a warm blanket. For extra warmth, the plastic garbage bag in your Altoid Survival Kit will act as extra insulation, should there be a blizzard or hurricane. Resist the urge to get out of your car in a harsh snowstorm and walk for help.

Always have a needle handy to use as an emergency compass

(floated in water on a leaf, the pointy part of the needle will face north).

Plus, with a little bit of thread,

you can sew a button back on!

YOUR SIGNATURE SCENT:
LEMON PERFUME

When we were young, my friend and cohort Andy Reinhardt and I used to hole up and create. Things. Experiments. Small masterpieces. Little-known works of great importance in the worlds of geography, cartography, and conceptual art. One of our early collaborations was a book, titled *Flags of the World*, which depicted original flag designs for some of the more obscure countries of the world, many of which you may not have ever heard of. Bing-Bing Loretta (on the Mediterranean Sea), the small principality of Chicken (we understood it to be near Turkey), and Bilogely (whose flag featured a vaguely bee-like animal) were just a few of the flags that we commissioned ourselves to design. Due to an imagined demand, we produced a similarly illustrated treatise called *Countries of the World*.

But our shining moment came with a simple experiment in alchemy, our foray into the creation and manufacture of perfume. One fragrance specifically: our custom-blended "Lemon Perfume." This unpretentious scent had top notes of tart lemon, rich middle notes of San Francisco tap water, and subtle bottom notes of L'Air du Temps, Je Reviens, or whatever leftover bouquet still haunted our mothers' old perfume bottles, which we used as containers.

There were faint rumblings during our first trials that the perfume felt "sticky." Apparently, our testers felt that "pulp and seeds" had no place in a fine perfume. It was going to take perseverance and faith in our vision to overcome those few thorny obstacles that plague the artistic soul. We would have to refine, create, fail, and fail again if we wanted to perfect our creation. But, clearly, we had other things to do, like going home because we had to do our homework, and our moms had to mix evening cocktails and make tuna casseroles.

But the dream never died, and so, today, I present to you the perfected, seedless variation of Mellor & Reinhardt's Original Lemon Perfume. A simple, refreshing scent you can make in the privacy of your kitchen and splash on during those hot summer days. And during tough economic times, you can wear this cologne with pride, knowing that it cost you the equivalent of a couple of double lattes.

MAKE YOUR OWN PERFUME:
MELLOR & REINHARDT'S LEMON PERFUME

INGREDIENTS

   3 ounces alcohol, either 190 proof alcohol or vodka (vodka!)

   2 tbsp finely chopped lemon peel

   1 tbsp finely chopped orange peel

   10 peppercorns, crushed

A handful of lemon and orange blossoms, if you have some
   growing
20 drops pure lemon essential oil
2 tbsp distilled water
½ ounce fixative, which prolongs a fragrance. They lend
   their own unique scent and help retard the evaporation
   of your scent. Commonly used fixatives are essential
   oils of sandalwood, benzoin, myrrh, and vanilla
Eyedroppers
Small glass vials, bottles, jars

Combine the vodka, fruit peels, peppercorns, and blossoms
in a jar. Cover and let stand in a dark spot for 1 week. Strain the
liquid through cheesecloth into a clean jar and add the essential
oil to the liquid. Let stand for 2 to 6 weeks, shaking the jar
once a day. When the scent is where you want it to be, add the
distilled water and fixative. Keep in a dark bottle or in a cool,
dark area.

You can try adding herbs, coffee beans, cloves, or a
cinnamon stick to your lemon peels to add some complexity to
your lemon scent. Strain along with the peels.

You can also make your own easy perfume with pure essential oils, for which you will need:

Your favorite pure essential oils (such as rose, lavender,
   jasmine, clove, vetiver, sandalwood, patchouli)
3 ounces alcohol, either 190 proof alcohol or vodka
2 tbsp distilled water

½ ounce fixative (essential oils of sandalwood, benzoin,
     myrrh, or vanilla)
Eyedroppers
Small glass vials, bottles, jars

Add the jojoba oil or sweet almond oil to the bottle with an
eyedropper. Add the alcohol and 20 to 30 drops of your favorite
essential oils. Experiment with various combinations.

Clean the eyedropper in alcohol or vodka between each
addition of a new essential oil. Shake the bottle for a couple of
minutes, then let it sit for 48 hours to 6 weeks in a cool, dry,
dark area. The scent will change over time. Aging your formula
is necessary to blend and mellow the scent. Check the scent
after a few days to see where you might make adjustments. It
will be strongest after about six weeks.

When the scent is where you want it to be, add the distilled
water to the perfume. Shake the bottle to mix the perfume,
then filter it through a coffee filter and pour it into its final
bottle. Ideally, this will be a dark bottle with minimal airspace,
since light and exposure to air degrade many essential oils.

You can pour a little perfume into a decorative bottle, but in
general, store your perfume in a dark sealed bottle, away from
heat and light. Keep track of the date and ingredients, in case you
want to duplicate your creation. Give it a kicky name!

For an oil-based scent, use jojoba oil, which is odorless and
lasts a long time. Almond oil also works well as a base. As a basic
recipe, mix 1 ounce jojoba or sweet almond oil to 15 to 20 drops
of essential oils. Try a mixture of jasmine oil and rose, with a
drop or two of vanilla. Cover and shake. The scent will change

over time, so test it on your forearm after a few weeks, and make necessary adjustments.

Sometimes you just have to look at
where you are, and think to yourself,
I AM THE LUCKIEST GIRL IN THE WORLD

FACIAL MASSAGE: CAN A MILLION CZECHS BE WRONG?

Glowing Eastern European skin-care specialists believe in it, and so do I. Anti-aging experts say it will tone and contour, erase wrinkles, and impart a youthful glow. They are certainly right about the youthful glow, and if nothing else it will boost your circulation, ease sinus pressure, and just feel really, really good. And don't stop at your face! Your scalp can take much heavier pressure than the delicate facial skin, so give your scalp a good, hearty rub to really make it tingle. It's something we can do ourselves, daily, for free!

The skin on your face is fragile, so massage it with a light touch and gentle pressure. You will need a base of cold-pressed vegetable oil; I like olive, safflower, or coconut. About one teaspoon in a small, clean bowl will be enough for a single massage. Pour the oil into the palm of your clean hand, rub your hands together, and apply over your face and neck.

Forehead: Begin in the middle of the forehead, making small circular movements out toward the temples.

Eyes: From your temples, glide your index fingers over your brow and circle your eye sockets. The pressure should be very light.

Nose: Slide your fingers down each side of your nose to the tip and up again. End at the top of the mouth.

Mouth: Use your index and middle fingers and start at the chin, gently massaging in a circular and upward motion around the mouth and lips. Bring the massage motion to the top of the mouth, under the nostrils.

Cheeks: In a circular motion, massage outward from your chin to your earlobes, from the corners of your mouth to the middle of your ears and from your nostrils to your temples. Cover the whole cheek area.

Chin: Beginning on your right, where the jaw meets your ear, using your thumb and index finger, gently slide across the jaw to your chin. Massage back to the starting point with circular motions. Repeat on the left side.

Neck: Beginning at the back of the neck, massage upward to the head with small, circular motions. Come around to the front of the neck and gently stroke upward from the collarbone to the jawline. With loose, elastic fingers, proceeding from the jawline to the chin, do gentle pinching movements across the chin, to the cheeks. Then, using your middle, fourth, and baby fingers, make gentle, circular, uplifting motions on the cheeks and around the nose. Massage around the nose area up to the stress area between the eyes.

NATURAL HOME REMEDIES

Cockroach Killer: Mix equal parts of boric acid powder and sugar. The sugar attracts the cockroaches, and they take it back to their roach dens and think they're really getting away with something, and then they're totally surprised when they die of boric acid poisoning. It's diabolical! You can pour this mixture into jar lids or little shallow bowls and place in the areas where you believe your cockroaches may be taking up residence, such as behind the refrigerator or underneath the kitchen sink. Sprinkling it along cracks in the floorboards is effective, as well as in dark, cockroach-friendly corners. Do not place this mixture on kitchen or bathroom counters or floors, or in your children's cereal bowl or in your dog's food dish.

Homemade Furniture Polish: Combine two parts olive oil with one part apple cider vinegar or white vinegar. (You can use lemon juice, too, but you'll have to keep it in the fridge.) Add some lemon oil or vanilla extract to give it a less vinegar-y scent. Put into a spray bottle and label. Use as a polish for finished (not raw or unfinished) wood. Shake it up to mix, spray on a soft cloth, and polish.

Insect Repellent: Mix a few drops of peppermint or lavender essential oil with a few drops of essential oil of lemon and two teaspoons of almond oil and dab at the ankles, wrists, and wherever else you fear insects might come around.

Bug-free Picnic Table: Add ten drops of lavender essential oil to a quart of water in a spray bottle. Spray and wipe down the table and chairs.

A Really Good Picnic Trick: Fill up a few empty, rinsed milk cartons (not quite to the top) with filtered water and freeze. Use the frozen cartons to keep food chilled in your ice chest. When the ice blocks melt, you can use them for drinking water! Good for earthquakes and apocalypses, too!

VARIOUS USES FOR ESSENTIAL OILS AND KITCHEN HERBS

It helps to have an eyedropper for the following recipes. Clean your eyedropper in between uses by squeezing some alcohol or vodka up into the dropper.

- Shake a few drops of oil of lavender or your favorite essential oil on a small piece of cloth or handkerchief. Throw this into the dryer when you are drying a load of clothes. Instant scented dryer sheet!

- Boil a handful of cloves in a pot of water to make the house smell delicious.

- Add ten drops of orange oil or lavender oil to a box of baking soda. Mix it well, and let the mixture sit for a day or two. Sprinkle on your carpets, leave it to sit for an hour or two, then vacuum. You may also put a few drops onto a cotton ball, vacuum up the cotton ball, and release the scent as you vacuum.

- Lay a piece of plastic wrap into shoes. Put a few drops of clove, geranium, or lemon essential oil on a cotton ball and place it on plastic wrap to remove the odor. (Remove before wearing, duh.) If you have a couple of mesh tea balls around the house, use them as shoe fresheners! Put a drop or two of essential oil on a cotton ball, place the cotton inside the tea ball and put the tea ball inside your shoe. Repeat with your other stinky shoe.

- Hungover? I've heard that essential oils of juniper, cedarwood, grapefruit, lavender, carrot, fennel, rosemary, and lemon may help blunt the effects of overindulging. Make your own blend of these oils and place eight to ten drops in a bath. Or place a few drops on a soft cloth, which you can place over your face while "resting your eyes."

- Blend equal parts jojoba oil with tea tree essential oil. Use as a skin soother, and when you have problem pimples. In the bath, massage it gently all over your face after cleansing. Let it sit on your face while you bathe.

- In the winter, during flu season, place the peels of a few lemons and a handful of thyme along with a few drops of lemon and thyme essential oils into a large pot of water. Let simmer on the stove.

- A few drops of peppermint oil diluted with a teaspoon of olive or almond oil and rubbed on the back of the neck and temples will help relieve a headache.

- Dilute eight to ten drops of eucalyptus oil in a cup of whole milk. Add to your bath. Imagine you're Claudette Colbert as Cleopatra having her milk bath.

- A drop of two of lavender on your wrists before bed will help you sleep. Likewise, a drop or two of lavender, chamomile, marjoram, or neroli on your pillow will promote a dreamy sleep.

- Essential oils of vetiver, cypress, frankincense, and myrrh all make wonderful scents for your fireplace fire. Drop approximately four drops on a dried log. Let the oil soak in before putting the log on the fire.

- Blend geranium, lavender, and bergamot to alleviate
anxiety and depression. Dilute eight drops in a half-
cup of whole milk, and add to your bath.

- To make bath salts, combine three cups of Epsom
salts, one tablespoon of glycerin, and several drops
of your favorite essential oils, such as peppermint,
bergamot, rose, or lavender, in a glass or metal bowl.
Put half a cup or more of the mixture into the hot
bath. Store the rest in an apothecary jar with a lid.

- For a nice hair treatment, add a few drops of lavender
oil or rosemary oil to a tablespoon of warm (not
boiling) castor or sweet almond oil. Massage into
your scalp and apply to the ends of your hair. Then
wrap your hair with plastic wrap or a plastic shower
cap and cover with a warm towel— warm the towel
quickly by tossing it into the dryer for a few minutes.
Or sit out in the sunshine and let the sun warm your
oily head. Be sure to wave to your neighbors!

- "Virgin's Milk is compounded with tincture of Benzoin
and Rose-water; it is prepared by simply adding a few
drops of the former to an ounce or two of the latter,
which produces a milky mixture. If the face be washed
with this, it will give it a beautiful ivory color. Let it
remain on the skin without wiping."

(From *Toilette of Rank and Fashion,* published in 1837)

And why not? I'll try it if you will.

Use your hair conditioner on your legs
As a great, soothing shaving cream.

I am not kidding about the HONEY on your face
It is a natural humectant
Which is a good thing

Squeeze two lemons into half a cup of water, then splash over face and rinse. Lemon juice contains alpha hydroxy acid, which dissolves dead skin and fights bacteria, so the concoction helps banish blemishes.

SLEEP IN HEAVENLY PEACE

YOU MAY HAVE NOTICED CERTAIN THINGS CHANGING AS YOU grow up into an age you used to think of as "old." But now, we laugh at your twenty, we spit on your thirty, we see your forty and raise you ten. We are smart, fascinating, wise, powerful, fabulous women. Also, sleepy. Very sleepy, tired, not-getting-enough-sleep women. Waking-up-many-times-a-night women. Want sleep. More. Sleep.

We hear that less than seven or eight hours can lead to heart disease, a flabby belly, and a generally impaired life. But it's just not that easy to get the whole seven to eight hours. Some of us are former night owls, and find those quiet hours after the family has dropped sweetly off into slumber-land some of the best hours to get stuff done. Some of us are discovering that hormonal changes can cause alarming symptoms, making us throw off the covers in the middle of the night because of a sudden and overwhelming wave of heat, then, fifteen minutes later, pull the covers back on, then off again an hour later. And so on. Some of us can't sleep through the din of a tiny creaking noise at the far end of the house, much less our partner's snoring. Some of us just find ourselves *wide awake* the minute our head hits the pillow at eleven P.M., even though we were so tired at six we could barely keep our eyes open. Things have gone kind of bonky, but we're not yet ready to begin a regimen of Ambien, Lunesta, or other pharmaceuticals to help us sleep. Or perhaps some of us tried a half an Ambien once, and we woke up feeling as if we'd been heavily drugged, hit on the head several times, and carried off to the slave traders who put us to sleep underwater. It was perhaps not the most restorative night.

The following remedies are old-fashioned, but tried and true; and all surprisingly helpful.

Hot bath and herbal tea. Get into a bath that's as hot as you can stand it. For extra relaxation, add some Epsom salts and a few drops of lavender essential oil. Drink the hot herbal tea while you're in the bath. This is also an excellent remedy should you be feeling slightly under the weather. Soak for at least ten minutes, more if you can manage. Put on something cozy after you've dried off, and climb into bed.

Earplugs. Oh. My. God. Earplugs. May we take a moment here and give praise to the person who came up with those ingenious foam earplugs? They're a little weird at first, because you really cannot hear anything once you insert them, and when you're used to hearing leaves falling in the backyard, or the icemaker in your refrigerator kicking into action, or the sound of your child breathing softly from down the hall, then it's more than a little disconcerting to suddenly be hearing nothing but the swishing sounds of your own brain. Or whatever it is that's swishing. It's like floating in deep space.

Simply twist the ends until they're pointy, and insert the plugs while tugging your earlobe gently with the opposite hand. The plugs will proceed to expand inside your ear, a process that sounds like a lot of paper crunching, or a small fire crackling inside your head. And then . . . silence. You can't even hear it when you climb into bed. Nothing! And I am telling you, utter silence is very, very sleep-inducing. The experience will be enhanced if you put soft flannel or jersey sheets on your bed, and, of course, a few drops of lavender on your wrists and pillow. Just the (yawn) thought of it . . . makes me (yawn! Sorry) . . . feel so cozy. I think I'll just rest my eyes for a minute.

Warning: you may not hear the alarm in the morning.

Valerian root. I have been known to take one capsule an hour before bed, or this great stuff called SLEEP ("Wake up refreshed, not fatigued!") available at Whole Foods Market, which also has its own version: just as effective but half the price.

Lavender oil. Dab on your wrist and behind your ears, and sprinkle on your pillow. Make a sachet of fresh lavender and place beside your bed and under your pillow.

The faint sound of your radio. This requires the consent of your sleep partner, if you have one, but if you generally like listening to the radio, and if you have a radio next to your bed, turn the radio on to your favorite talk station; preferably nothing too vitriolic or shrill. A nice, steady NPR discussion about a Wisconsin sheep's-cheese farm, or something. Turn the radio to the lowest possible volume, so you can barely hear it. Then lie there, all cozy in your bed, and as you strain to hear the radio, you will fall asleep. I do this when I want to go back to sleep on a

Sunday morning, for instance. I've been doing this for years, but recently my friend Geri, who is always full of helpful tips, piped up at dinner one night with the information she just read somewhere that listening to a radio at a very low volume is a surefire sleep inducer. What do you know?!

THE BEST SLEEP TRICK EVER

For this particular exercise, you will need to enlist the help of a friend or loved one. Preferably a friend or loved one who knows a little bit about the game of golf. One night, many years ago, I was feeling anxious, restless, wide-awake, and unable to sleep. I had to get to sleep, because I had to work the next day, and so my husband sat down next to me on the bed, and he stroked my head, and he told me to shut my eyes and take a few deep, full breaths. And then he started telling me, in a very low, soothing voice, about a golf game he had recently played. He used to play golf, and had a very love/hate relationship with the game. But he knew how to talk about it. So he sat on the edge of the bed and began describing a recent game, or maybe it was a game he was making up on the fly; but it goes like this:

"The first hole is a three-hundred-ninety-yard par four dogleg to the right. There are trees along the right side of the fairway, so it's safest to aim a little to the left, even though that's the wrong direction to the green. In the past I've played it left and gone way left, out of bounds, and I've also tried to play it to the right along the trees and gotten into trouble there. I don't need too much length so I choose to tee off with my three-wood instead of my driver just to keep it straight. Standing over the ball on the first tee I know everyone is judging me—not only the people I'm playing with but the people waiting to tee off behind me—it's best to relax, stay in rhythm, and not try to hit the ball too hard. I end up taking a good swing and somehow hitting a decent shot. I nonchalantly pick up my tee and let my friend tee off.

"The stroll to ball is friendly and familiar. When I reach my ball I find it sitting up nicely in the grass on the fairway, and I have another one hundred and seventy yards to the green. There's a hill between me and the hole, so I can't see the flagstick or the green. Having been here before I know if I hit my four-iron properly, I'll get there—if I'm a little short it's okay because the ball can kick off the hill and onto the green. Long is no good because there are woods directly behind the green. Today, however, I have some wind at my back. I'm thinking maybe even a five-iron could get there. I take out the five-iron and swing it a little, debating whether it's worth the risk. My friend's ball is fairly close to me and he hits first. He hits a lovely shot but it only makes it to the top hill—he's short of the green by ten yards—I ask him what club he hit and he says a five-iron. He looks stunned. I'm thinking I would have to be an idiot to hit the same club. I have to hit a four-iron to reach the green. In the past the four has proven to be the right club from this distance and it's better to swing easily with the four than trying to crush the five-iron. At least that's what I keep telling myself. Ultimately I swing easy, but I swing so easy that I hit the ball off the heel of the club—the ball doesn't get the proper loft and hits the hill in front of the green, shortening the shot and leaving me another twenty yards to the green.

"When I reach my ball on the other side of the hill, I can see that the hole is on the front of the green so my third shot is a slightly downhill pitch that I must land in front of the green and hope the ball runs to the pin. The grass is thick around the green's apron and the ball could get caught up in it, but if I land the ball on the green it will run for another thirty feet away from the hole so I have to play it just right. Normally I'm good with these pitch shots and I can picture it before I even hit it. This time in fact I perform the task about as well as a pro and end about seven feet away from the hole, putting for a par.

"I line up the putt. I know this green. I know this putt. I've hit this putt. It will bend a little to the right just as it gets to the hole. This is going to be a sweet par considering I hit a conservative tee shot, and a crummy second shot. The third shot, however, was a classy piece of work, now I just have to make it mean something by sinking the putt. I stand over ball thinking that I've got to aim to the left, but not too far to the left. I don't want to hit too hard 'cause it could run four or five feet away. Ultimately I panic a little and hit the putt a little weak and I'm thinking, 'oh no I left it short,' and then it just falls in the right edge of the hole. I smile, feign wiping perspiration off my forehead, pluck my ball from the hole, and head to the second tee . . ."

. . . And on it goes. Much like that. In a gentle, dulcet tone of voice. Whenever I get the golf-story sleep treatment, I am apparently asleep before the first green.

You may want to have your husband, friend, or loved one read the above passage in a soft and tranquil tone, or find a friend with some actual golf experience and ask them to pop over and give you their own play-by-play when you're having trouble sleeping. Better yet, make a recording of their golf-game story, so you can whip it out anytime you're having a rough night. Make sure they describe one of their more dull games. No holes-in-one, colorful language, or surprising golf-related events. This should not be difficult, as exciting golf stories are the exception rather than the rule. You might want to give yourself a few options: nine holes for your average insomnia, eighteen holes for those nights when you mistakenly had coffee too late in the day. You might want to make an audio recording of the Golf Channel some Sunday afternoon, to use in a pinch.

The hot bath, hot tea, and a little lavender sachet doesn't hurt either, but there is no more guaranteed soporific than listening to every teeny-tiny detail of a seemingly interminable golf game.

Fore, baby! And sweet dreams.